Chain Reaction

How Today's Best Companies Manage Their Supply Chains for Superior Performance

Chain Reaction

How Today's Best Companies Manage Their Supply Chains for Superior Performance

Robert A. Malone

KAPLAN) PUBLISHING

New York

This publication is designed to provide accurate and authoritative information in regard to the subject matter covered. It is sold with the understanding that the publisher is not engaged in rendering legal, accounting, or other professional service. If legal advice or other expert assistance is required, the services of a competent professional should be sought.

Vice President and Publisher: Maureen McMahon
Editorial Director: Jennifer Farthing
Acquisitions Editor: Shannon Berning
Development Editor: Siobhán McKiernan Flahive
Production Editor: Karina Cueto
Production Artist: PBS & Associates
Cover Designer: Jodie Billert

© 2007 by Robert A. Malone

Published by Kaplan Publishing, a division of Kaplan, Inc.
1 Liberty Plaza, 24th Floor
New York, NY 10006

All rights reserved. The text of this publication, or any part thereof, may not be reproduced in any manner whatsoever without written permission from the publisher.

Printed in the United States of America

September 2007
10 9 8 7 6 5 4 3 2 1

ISBN-13: 978-1-4195-9681-0

Kaplan Publishing books are available at special quantity discounts to use for sales promotions, employee premiums, or educational purposes. Please email our Special Sales Department to order or for more information at kaplanpublishing@kaplan.com, or write to Kaplan Publishing, 1 Liberty Plaza, 24th Floor New York, NY 10006.

DEDICATION

To Norbert Wiener
His development of the concept of "feedback" became the core of a consumer pull economy.

Contents

Introduction ix

PART ONE
WORLD REALITIES

1. WONDERLAND: THE WORLD'S NEW SCALE 3

2. CHOREOGRAPHING SURVIVAL: RISK AND ADAPTATION 17

3. REALITY CRUNCH: OUR PERCEPTIONS AND REACTIONS 31

4. LEONARDO FLUNKED LATIN: INNOVATING AND INVENTING 39

5. FIVE-MINUTE PLAN: ENHANCING BUSINESS PROCESSES 51

6. DEUS EX MACHINA: THE GROWTH OF AUTOMATION 61

7. THE WORLD IS ALWAYS WITH US: COMMUNICATION 71

PART TWO
SUPPLY CHAIN EVOLUTION

8. THE HISTORY OF THE SUPPLY CHAIN 85

9. LIFT THAT BALE: TRANSPORT BY GROUND, AIR, SEA, AND RAIL 97

10. PINS TO PORSCHES: THE EVOLUTION OF MANUFACTURING   117

11. ACTIVITY NOT PLACE: OUTSOURCING   131

12. SILKS TO CELLS: RETAIL EVOLUTION   143

13. THE STORE'S THE THING: RETAILING AND THE SUPPLY CHAIN   149

14. PORTS, SHIPS, HUBS, AND RAILS: INTERMODAL TRANSPORTATION   161

15. A MILLION SQUARE FEET OF CHOCOLATE: WAREHOUSING AND DISTRIBUTION CENTERS   175

PART THREE
SUPPLY CHAIN RESOLUTION

16. WHAT'S MISSING? SUPPLY CHAIN CHALLENGES   185

17. PYRAMIDS TO PARAMECIUMS: SUPPLY CHAIN MODELING   197

18. MAKING IT RIGHT: A GLOBAL PERSPECTIVE   213

19. AN ATLAS ACT: REPAIRING THE GLOBAL SUPPLY CHAIN   221

20. BY INTELLIGENT RESPONSE: THE FUTURE   231

Acknowledgements   243
Index   245
About the Author   255

Introduction

LOGISTICS TO THE HORIZON

One fine, brisk fall afternoon I was invited by an Asian shipping company to visit the Port of New York and New Jersey. Most ships coming to this port are foreign owned. There are almost no international trade ships bearing the U.S. flag. The date of my visit was exactly 50 years after the first container-laden ship left this very port bound for Houston, Texas, under the direction of the late Malcolm McLean, the creator of the now-famous steel box shipping container. It is often called "the box" and is the principal means of distribution in the world.

Walking up the five-story gangway gave some measure of the ship's size (longer, wider, and higher than the *Titanic*). We had breakfast in the galley; the crew consisted of mariners from all over the world. They represented the new face of the world's supply chains: foreign born, bred, and paid.

TO THE BRIDGE

On the ship's bridge, up several decks via an elevator, I watched while stevedores unloaded containers from the ship to the dock. The bridge of this type of vessel is 105 feet wide, a critical figure because the Panama Canal, at 110 feet wide, is just slightly wider. New ships may be 20 feet wider.

In a vast panorama, the port with its endlessly stacked containers, swinging cranes, huge terminals, and docked ships was set against an even larger view of the New Jersey Turnpike and Newark Airport. The major highway artery was teeming with big rigs. At Newark Airport, both cargo and passenger planes were taking off and landing.

Using binoculars, I could identify the FedEx jets in the distance; read the lengths of shipping containers printed on their ends (some 53 feet long); and watch huge rolling, four-story straddle carriers trundling along in the port's background, having taken containers to their proper place. Some of the containers were "reefers," or refrigerated containers, which require special handling because they are plugged into the ship when aboard and into land connections when docked. Nobody wants melted shrimp after a four-day voyage at sea.

The port moved over four million containers in 2003. That's over 1,000 each day—and the numbers have only increased since this figure was released. More than 130 million tons of bulk cargo move in and out of this port annually: Toyota and BMW cars, IKEA furniture, raw materials such as chemicals, and loads of waste paper.

Let's place the Port of New York and New Jersey in a logistics context. Logistics is the process of physically transporting and tracking goods, and in the United States in 2005, it represented nearly 10 percent of the GDP, or $1.763 trillion. It is important to know that the Port of New York and New Jersey is the third largest in the nation, after Los Angeles and Long Beach, California. These two California ports together see nearly three times the volume of containers that the Port of New York and New Jersey does. But the three U.S. ports combined don't hold a candle to Singapore and other Asian ports.

Port	Containers per year*	Bulk cargo per year*
Singapore	21 million plus	347 million tons plus
Hong Kong	21 million plus	207 million tons plus
Shanghai	14 million plus	316 million tons plus
Los Angeles	7 million plus	N/A
Long Beach	5.7 million	62 million tons plus
NY/NJ	4 million plus	132 million tons plus

* 2004 figures

LOST HORIZONS

While at the port, I took a moment to look at the venerable Bayonne Bridge, southeast of the port. This is the arch bridge that spans from Staten Island to Bayonne, New Jersey. It is the gateway to the docks of Elizabeth and Newark that constitute the Port of New York and New Jersey. The bridge is too low to accommodate the new containerships already plying the weighs and far too small for those now being designed. These new ships are classified as post-Panamax, meaning beyond the specifications of the Panama Canal.

The Port of New York and New Jersey is therefore at risk because the Bayonne Bridge is the gateway to the port. The last major bridge built in New York was the Verrazano-Narrows, completed in 1964. Building a bridge in the New York area today would be as difficult as building a new World Trade Center; it would take 10 years if things go well. World trade will not wait that long.

The biggest U.S. port, Los Angeles, has no more real estate. That means that it is, for all intents and purposes, frozen in time and inadequate for any future development without major political and economic upheaval. Despite these and other challenges, however, I am not saying that smart U.S. companies cannot perform superlatively in regard to their supply chains and meet the demands of consumers. They can and they do.

HARDENING OF UNCLE SAM'S ARTERIES

Newark and Elizabeth are often referred to as the armpit, or worse, of the region. The cranes of the port are old and need replacement. Trucks must wait about two hours to pick up containers. The access roads are jammed. The port has recently been dredged, but even if more traffic could come in by ship, the port has limited storage space and nowhere to expand. It is possible that several smaller facilities such as Red Hook in Brooklyn and Howland Hook on Staten Island can take up slack; however, Red Hook is an unprofitable facility and is slated for removal, and Howland Hook has limited capacity and very tightly held expansion space. I'll have more to say on this later when I cover facilities.

FORTUNE COOKIES

In 2005, the United States exported $34.7 billion worth of goods to China, while China exported $196.6 billion worth of goods to the United States. Of every 100 shipping containers that come to the United States, 60 return to China empty. A decade ago, that number was 16. Shippers of such cargo charge around $200 per empty container in addition to the actual cost of shipping. A full container costs six or seven times as much.

In the trade, this is referred to as the problem of "empties." The bulk of the full containers that are sent back to China from the United States are crammed with waste paper. Other unexpected exports to China from the United States are scrap metal and hay. In 2005, the Chinese GDP was more than $2 trillion, while the GDP of the United States was over $12 trillion, or about six times China's GDP—and yet we have a trade imbalance.

BIG BOX CONSUMES MCLEAN BOXES

Wal-Mart alone imported 695,000 shipping containers into the United States in 2005. That is equal to more than one container a minute. Most of these Wal-Mart–directed containers come from Chinese manufacturers and travel via a U.S. distribution center (about 1,000,000 square feet in size) to U.S. stores filled with U.S. shoppers and many, many Wal-Mart associates. If you shop at Wal-Mart, Bed Bath & Beyond, The Home Depot, or a similar large retailer, you will find you are basically buying Chinese wares. It is unusual to find a product made in the United States.

Are we waking a sleeping dragon with China, or is the dragon already awake? The scale of huge distribution centers may lead to new problems; very large systems are large opportunities to make large mistakes. These retailers' investments in real estate and bricks and mortar occur as the economy shifts more and more toward the Internet and electronic trade.

Shippers and retailers in the United States may believe that our superpower status is independent of our trade situation. We are probably feeding the dragon, which may one day have us as a meal. The United States is the world's second largest exporter after Germany, which has about one-fourth the population. However, the United States is the world's largest importer, and our gluttony may catch up with us.

In the pages ahead, I will address the supply chain and its implications to business in three parts. First, I will examine how the changing realities of our world have refashioned our methods of survival and business adaptation—and how the new methodologies of automation and communication require a new look at innovation and business strategies.

I will follow this with a review of where the concepts of logistics and the supply chain come from, and how these concepts are being applied by companies successful in logistics, manufacturing, and retailing. I will explain how warehouses are being transformed into distribution centers, and why.

Finally, I will look at the best means of defining (modeling) the supply chain as dynamic, organic, and built to deliver the best response to the customer and to the bottom line.

Part One

WORLD REALITIES

Time marches on, but the pace of time is not a constant. Technology evolves within time at various speeds. We happen to be in an era of rapid, revolutionary change, both technological and strategic. Our space-time continuum now includes nanotechnology, faster and faster computing, and the generation of information from data at a scale that has never been seen before. At the same time that our tools and machines operate at a miniscule scale, they are also operating at a gigantic scale, as with our containerships.

Chapter

1

WONDERLAND: THE WORLD'S NEW SCALE

Like Lewis Carroll's Alice, we in the 21st century have figuratively fallen down a rabbit hole into a Wonderland not exactly to our specifications. It is a compendium of many complex and powerful technological forces.

We are not as we have been. We now walk around on the street talking, as if to ourselves, when, in fact, we are actually talking to the babysitter via a wireless earpiece connected to our cell phones. We know where we are and where we are going courtesy of our GPS systems; we signal our cars with our keys, they answer with a beep, and the doors automatically unlock. Some people wear pacemakers, others artificial hips or knees. We are becoming more robot-like than we would like to acknowledge. We constantly operate with assists. If you want to immobilize some people, take away their cell phone, PDA, and MP3 player, which may now all be contained in one device. We use our home phones to call our cell phones in order to find them buried under the soiled laundry. We have more computing power in our home offices than NASA's Apollo missions used to get to the moon.

EARTH IS OBLATE STILL

Even Alice knew the words *latitude* and *longitude,* our means of describing Earth's spherical nature. The Earth itself is more or less round, and is the same basic diameter as when Galileo lived.

It is our communication around it and our transportation of people and goods about the Earth that have changed. What has changed are the scale, the speed of human travel, the speed of communication, and the availability of automated tools and systems to nearly everyone, almost everywhere.

Almost everything is faster, and this makes the world seem smaller—more local. We are all, in a way, in each other's faces, for better or for worse. Regardless of physical distance, people are a cell phone call or an email message away from one another. Information that once took months or weeks to travel now takes only days, hours, or less than a second. We are informed as no other generation has been informed.

We live under the illusion that we are receiving information in real time; however, only information communication closes in upon real time, and "closes in" is the right term. The movement of goods is faster than in the past, but still is not instantaneous. At airports we wait, often with our shoes off. While airfreight may have become faster, air travel is often slower than an old local bus. Goods are physical and still require time-conscious handling because of their bulk, while data is compressible and communicable almost instantly.

INFORMATION OBESITY?

Like it or not, we have to get used to a new world scale. Even if we are sitting on an old bus, we still live in a world that now recognizes and uses information of vast proportions.

An exabyte is 1,000,000,000,000,000,000 bytes (a byte is eight bits, and a bit is a value of either 1 or 0). An exabyte is therefore very, very large. If you find yourself with time on your hands, you can multiply all of the information in the Library of Congress by 57,000 and reach a figure of eight exabytes. All human spoken words in history are calculated to be five exabytes.

Information in magnetic media (e.g., digital information from business such as bar code readers, robot vision systems, and financial software) accounts for more than 90 percent of this staggering total. The University of California at Berkeley study that calculated some of these figures estimates that global information increases about 30 percent per year. Get a handle on that factoid! It can be hard to tell whether this is really information obesity, or just a new and normal state of our times.

An exabyte is important to us because knowing anything now takes new tools. The old tools have serious limitations of volume and, consequently, of our ability, in time, to take in and use the information they hold. The introduction of graphics and digital documents into our work would have overwhelmed earlier computer systems. We send pictures by email or cell phone now without a second thought.

Most people are used to the scales of kilobytes (1,000 bytes), megabytes, gigabytes (the storage capacity of personal computers is measured in gigabytes), and terabytes (new data warehouses are measured in terabytes). Businesspeople will have to become willing to think in terabytes (1,000,000,000 bytes) and petabytes (1,000 terabytes) and to see these figures in the context of exabytes. Terabyte scales of information are the new standard for information servers dealing with large relational databases in corporations and governments. I believe that logistics and the global supply chain are fueling this move to unprecedented quantities of information.

There is a logistics and supply chain angle to this discussion; that is, petabytes do meet bar codes at Wal-Mart. The world of logistics with its new radio frequency identification data (RFID) compliance requirements, and the supply chain with its thousands of suppliers and parts moving everywhere on our globe both require terabytes. Wal-Mart has mandated that its suppliers be compliant with RFID, and because it is the United States' largest retailer, this is serious business. Wal-Mart recorded over $285 billion in sales in 2005, with more than 1.6 million associates and 3,700 stores in the United States. The volume of its physical sales means that huge volumes of data have to be processed and digested.

The increasing volume of information has created a market for companies that can provide backup and storage. Some of the major players in the data warehousing server marketplace are IBM's Informix, Oracle, Teradata, SAS, and the new, and apparently trailblazing, Netezza. These firms work in a data warehousing market that accounted for $8.7 billion worldwide in 2005. They are the new memory of business.

A company such as Google uses an enormous number of servers to process terabyte loads of information. Google receives more than 2,000 queries a second and can scan its 3 billion (and growing) Web pages in half a second. Googling is fast. It is faster than going to the public library. Instead we can go to Starbucks and google. Value added is big. Innovation is big. Innovative collaboration leading to added value is bigger.

There would be no Google without servers and their ability to process gobs of data. But let me get on to nanometers.

WHY NANOMETERS?

If you can get past exabytes, you may be ready for nanometers. A nanometer is a billionth of a meter. Just as a byte is the division of data, a nanometer is the division of matter.

First, let's get a better handle, if possible, on a nanometer. A nanometer is to a meter as a very small marble is to the Earth. That is very small! A human hair is about 80,000 nanometers wide. It shouldn't therefore be so hard to split hairs.

We have to get used to thinking in miniature, because of firms such as IBM; individuals such as K. Eric Drexler; and communities such as the University of California at Berkeley, the Weizmann Institute in Israel, the University of Wisconsin at Madison, and the 13 research universities being funded by the National Nanotechnology

Infrastructure Network. They are building, or preparing to build, devices at a nanometer level.

The advent of nano tools means that we will see, in the near future, computing devices, sensors, valves, motors, microflaps, positioning devices, and communication products of an infinitesimal size. Many of these will be working together within products that we may not, even when brought all together, be able to see even with specialized equipment, as they may be moving or changing at such a rate that we will need a pause button. To use them, we will have to have connection by wireless means.

They are making strides in that direction at Tokyo University. A researcher named Yuichi Hiratsuka has built a tiny micromotor using bacteria as the powering source. It is an integration of biological components into a microengineered system. The University of California at Los Angeles is in the process of building smart molecular computers one electron at a time. And even before nano tools become part of our everyday lives, the next step is already in sight: Researchers at Duke University are working on making objects not just small, but invisible to the eye.

BIG NANO

Miniaturization will change business. It will change logistics (transportation devices, cranes, fork lifts). It is already changing supply chains because nanotechnology resources are global. It will change the nature of security, privacy, and economics. Nanotechnology will usher in an era of intelligent products, materials, and environments. It will sadly also usher in a new level of risk to us all and to the supply chain.

Einstein warned us that the world is relative. I think what he meant by that was that time, motion, and mass are in a complex set of relationships to each other. The classic age of the past, when there were straight lines (not arcs), letters were delivered by letter carriers three times a day, and horse power was an actual horse, is gone.

Little things are not necessarily simple things: Miniaturization is already with us and might give us some indication of a nanotechnology world. An iPod Nano is a very small product that has hundreds of parts that are made all over the world and assembled in China and Mexico, yet it is known as a product of Apple Computer, Inc. of Cupertino, California. An iPod Nano is a wonder product in regard to its supply chain. An iPod itself is a supply chain. The final product may be more than the sum of its parts when the music is played, but it is a product that could not exist without the sources of the world.

It is so small yet so far reaching. It is a harbinger of many things to come. Electronic products are already getting smaller and smaller. A telephone on the front in World War I required about eight soldiers to carry it. A World War II walkie-talkie now seems refrigerator sized. Today a camera phone extends the limit of our thumb's capability. If you take a cell phone apart, you find layers of components that are unrecognizable to the layman.

Miniaturization is the inevitable direction of our technology, leading us to a nanometer world faster than many of us would care to believe. This move is coupled with an enlargement of our capacity to store and use information at an exabyte level.

The tools of logistics will be no exception to this rule: The working parts of trucks, ships, planes, and trains will be miniaturized and "nanotized." It is the new horizon for automation.

SIZE IS DECEIVING

Little things can now have big effects. Apple sold over 10 million iPods in one quarter of 2006. A new iPod can hold 15,000 songs or 25,000 photos. That's the equivalent of storage for 150,000,000,000 songs in a quarter of a year (or 600 billion in a year). Physically delivering that number of songs as sheet music or LPs, or delivering that number of photos after processing the film from Brownie cameras would have exhausted companies such as Columbia Records and Kodak, and all the delivery vans available.

And as we will see, a small local store or restaurant is really the product of big supply chains and logistics decisions that occur on a larger scale than we ever might have imagined.

MCDONALD'S IS A DELIVERY SYSTEM

Delivering meals today is information intensive, and when it becomes a global delivery, it encompasses logistics, currency exchange, customs, shipper specifications, partnerships, and contracts at a scale never before imagined. When we look at an individual store, such as a local McDonald's or Starbucks, that store is *it*. In fact, "it" must be multiplied by thousands to get a sense of the actual scale of its operations.

The sourcing of simple fare can girdle the globe. If I made a hamburger myself, it essentially would consist of ground beef and a bun. Yet McDonald's specifications for a Big Mac cover several pages in fine print and involve components from hundreds of suppliers. It is a chemical industry miracle, and a supply chain miracle. Big Mac ingredients are resourced as locally as possible, which means Big Macs have dozens or hundreds of supply chains behind them.

McDonald's essentially is a delivery system. The store is merely an extension of the supply chain. The patrons of McDonald's are also part of the supply chain as they use, separate, and dispose of millions of tons of paper and plastic.

Each day, McDonald's feeds the equivalent of the population of Spain. Each ingredient has to be resourced, sorted, packed, shipped, unpacked, sorted, cooked, fried, grilled, or shaken, and eventually eaten. In order to open McDonald's restaurants in Russia, the company had to start and run its own potato farms. Stores such as McDonald's appear to be the same eateries they were decades ago, but they are not. Appearance can hide the real workings and true complexity of today's businesses and their products.

CARS AS ROBOTS, TRUCKS AS COMMUNICATION CENTERS

The 1910 Ford Model T was less complex in its parts than a BMW's door is today, with its side airbag with occupant sensor, automatic rearview mirror control, automatic door locks that are heated and use a smart card or smart key for entry, door ajar warning, door entry light, and complete car window control. While products such as cars look similar to their early predecessors, they are not. What is important to note is that the Model T was a mechanical device that we called a car, and the new BMW is an electronic device that uses some mechanics that we still call a car. Cars are becoming robots that we sit in and, to some extent, control. They are no longer so much horseless carriages as they are automated motion platforms. There are more computers in a car than there are gears. Trucks are becoming moving warehouses with global positioning devices, wireless communication, fuel monitoring systems, and tire pressure sensors.

MORE

We have to get used to changes in our perception of volume (scale, size, and relative size). Each day around three million shipping containers are on the move. If all of them were lined end to end around the Earth, they would encircle the planet. The number of containers is increasing. Moving this volume of containers has enormous meaning to world trade; it essentially *is* world trade, except for airfreight and trucking.

There are 6.5 billion people living on Earth, a number that increases by about 200,000 each day (for an exact figure, visit *www.geohive.com*). In time that could be an increased demand for 200,000 more cell phones per day. About half of the world's population lives in five countries: China, India, the United States, Indonesia, and Brazil. India's population is growing the fastest. These are not physically the largest countries (those are Russia, Canada, and the United States); however, geographical size seems to have less and less to do with what is going on in the world. Right now, three of the four hottest spots for manufacturing are in China, and the other in India.

It may be difficult to get a sense of what 6.5 billion people do. They drive 54 million vehicles that use gas or diesel fuel. They operate over 2 billion cell phones, and around 900 million personal computers. About 200 million people use the Internet, and this figure grows by more than 10 percent each year. All of these products are made from many parts from many places and require many logistical processes. Many of these products are used in tandem: cell phones in cars (which themselves are composed of complex electronic parts and systems), or personal computers and the Internet. The use of the Internet can entail wireless communication with Earth satellites. Boy, do we need exabytes.

We are going two ways at once: an increase in information combined with complex products and tools that we can't see but may be able to control.

LIMITS TO SIZE?

"Form follows function" seems a reasonable idea, and yet if "form" includes the aspect of size, our present practices would appear to contradict this mandate.

Today's practice is often to disregard any limits of size on function's form. Big is therefore getting bigger every day. Look where you will; the big company is getting to be the bigger company, and the bigger retailer is getting to be the huge retailer. Wal-Mart, for instance, represents nearly 10 percent of all retail sales in the United States, and its corporate planning is aiming for 30 percent of U.S. sales. This should place everyone on notice.

The scaling up is not just one of actual size but one of virtual size as well. Little local airports with one runway seem to become international overnight. Cow colleges that used to teach young farm kids animal husbandry and how to raise juicy chickens are now universities with a big-name graduate school of business.

Globalism is the word of the day. To go global is most often praised, while to avoid the wonders of globalism is to risk being excoriated. Multinational is not enough: go global. The *New York Times* columnist Thomas Friedman is one of many suggesting that we can run global businesses while being paddled languourously in our Indonesian praus, our hand trailing in the silken waters with our cell phones tucked to the ear, or a light PDA in our laps. Anything is possible with the wonders of modern communication—or so we are led to believe. The old dictum "think global, act local" has been transformed into "think global and act global."

RIGHT SIZE

Size does matter. Recently a large snake in Florida tried to eat a rather large alligator. It died in the process. In California, Oracle has folded the company G-Log into its operation and thereby beefed up its logistics business. This is the latest in a long series of recent buyouts that still may not have satisfied the company's hunger. Can Oracle get too big and too defused? If we look around we find that SAP, IBM, Microsoft, and many others have that lean and hungry look. Will each of them be better for being bigger? What happens within each of the market pools when there are only a few giant enterprises, and they are still hungry?

In nature, as the large eat the small, the small replace themselves. In the business world, this may or may not be true. Are we producing as many small start-ups as we did in the 1990s? Are we starting new manufacturing companies to replace those that have given up in the face of competition in China? Are we still creating a wave of software start-ups to replace those that have disappeared by attrition or consumption or by being converted to programming outsource heaven India? Are there more or fewer initial public offerings (IPO) this year than last?

TWO-WAY STRETCH

We are experiencing a two-way stretch, but is the world ready? There is a stretch in the information column and a stretch in the column that represents the miniaturization and complexity of what we make and use. More and more things with more and more parts coming from more and more places need a more and more robust supply network and sophisticated logistics processing. We are going from a world where the few made things to a world where the many make things. Nations such as China, India, and Brazil, were minimally developed areas not long ago.

The implications for logistics and the supply chain are enormous: more people; more products; more shipments; more weight to shipments; and more demand for on-time delivery, fresh delivery, and delivery at all times packed, stacked, and tracked. The two-way stretch is operating on many levels.

A MOST DELIGHTFUL PARADOX

We are living in an age of contrasts and ironic juxtapositions. It is a paradoxical world. We have millions of computers that were supposed to give us a paperless world. The amount of paper being used continues to increase. U.S. consumption of uncoated free sheet paper increased at a rate of about 15 percent from 1995 to 2000. This was a period of intense increase in computer use, most particularly personal computer use.

Just as we consume more and more paper and compute more and more, smart electronic paper rears its unusual head. E Ink of Cambridge, Massachusetts, is developing a paperlike material that is flexible and readable. It has a silicon-based, thin-film transistor back plane. We've moved from a paper world to a supposed computer world to a mixed world to a world of silicon paper substitutes.

What does this mean for logistics? Well, it means today that trees, or wood pulp, are trucked, rail delivered, or water transported in massive quantities. Beyond the ugly figures of paper and pulp pollution, we have the ever-increasing need to move paper and waste paper globally. Some countries have plenty of trees; however, many don't. Countries that don't have paper, such as China (with few forests and an enormous need for paper), require huge inflows of pulp and paper or waste paper. This is the reason that so much of what the United States sends to China is waste paper and waste pulp.

COMPLEXITY GETS COMPLEX

Some artifacts or products continue to grow in complexity. These include space shuttles, communication satellites, nuclear reactor plants, and nuclear submarines. For instance, there are over 3,000,000 parts in a U.S. nuclear submarine. They all come from somewhere and have to be contracted for, manufactured, and tracked at each stage of their manufacture and transport. There are about 4,000,000 parts in a new Boeing 747. Boeing is just now beginning to use RFID tags on some of the more critical parts, as keeping up with tracking is otherwise impossible.

The Department of Defense (DoD) has its own ideas of a supply chain, and they are not simple, as a good deal is classified. It is little wonder that of the two first RFID mandates, DoD was one (Wal-Mart was the other). National security relies on the fact that the DoD knows where vital materials and parts are located worldwide.

COMPLEXITY IS IN THE NETWORK

The new complexity of manufacturing consists of products as large as trucks and as small as music players becoming assembly operations. Most, if not all, of the parts are made elsewhere. The corporations themselves are becoming complex as well to keep up with this new fluidity and the new global form of business. They are no longer principally confined to one location. They operate as networks. This is true for almost all big corporations. Central control gives way to decentralized control and yet centralized data keeping. A real corporation today is connected to other firms in a network. So a company is its networked partnerships, its collaborations, and its virtual companies.

EVEN SPEED IS GETTING FASTER

Speed of decision making is relative to the situation. The first moves in business, whether in an hourly, daily, or business quarter situation, are critical. All other decisions flow from the first. As speed gets faster, more decisions have to be made faster. Humans have limited capacity to increase their ability to speed their internal processing, so external tools have to come to the assistance—but these are not full substitutions for straight human processing. These tools include software processes such as business intelligence (BI) and business-assisted management (BAM).

SUMMING UP: WONDERLAND THROUGH THE LOOKING GLASS

Our world is a study in contrasts. Things are getting to be too many, too big, too fast, too few, too small, and too slow. We live and work in paradoxical circumstances. We either clasp firmly the new tools and strategies, or we sink into the netherworld and risk being passed off as of no consequence.

Chapter

2

CHOREOGRAPHING SURVIVAL: RISK AND ADAPTATION

SURVIVAL BY DESIGN

It is assumed that most people want to survive change and, if possible, to be prepared to meet risks with intelligence. They want to succeed, and in business this means one customer at a time. There is plenty of risk to go around these days, and managing risk has become infinitely more difficult today. It may be good to remember that yesterday's risk can become tomorrow's opportunity, while today's opportunity can become tomorrow's risk. It is only through measured risk that successful companies have been able to secure market advantage over their competitors. A company can meet the demand of a single customer only by the intelligent management of risk as part of the business process. We do not manage change. It is more that change manages us. We manage—when we are able—our response to change, and this response is what it is all about. It is the retailer's or manufacturer's or carrier's response to demand that governs success. Supply chain performance is often predicted by performance degradation that can be assigned to such events as the embargo of goods by a government, the closing down of a port by weather, or a sudden spike in fuel costs.

CHANGE IS WHAT IT WANTS TO BE

Change may be cyclical. It may be evolutionary. It may be by fits and starts. It may feel like a push forward, a push back, redemption, or destruction. Change can be perceived as a threat. Many see change (particularly technological change) as a threat to employment. Others may see change as a different type of threat. It can threaten long-held economic, social, and religious values.

Many methods exist to monitor and evaluate change such as a Pareto chart that is a means of rating quality in engineering process control. When the process exceeds or falls below the accepted range of values, this is an indicator that something may be wrong. A change can become an error, and an error can lead to risk, such as the risk of a poorly made part or product. The same can be said of a change in delivery time within the supply chain. A substantial change can lead to the risk of missing the demand entirely.

CHANGE IN WAVES

Manufacturing has gone through waves of change, with three changing phases: process mechanization and process power, process control and information processing, and, finally (or until today), process integration and the supply chain process.

Although each of these phases may lead to the next, this does not mean that what goes before is of no consequence. To the contrary; this is a history of accumulation and refinement, not a history of simple replacement. For example, the discovery in the first phase (late 18th century) of interchangeable parts is as useful today as it was then. The parts have changed, the processing of the parts has changed, but interchangeability may remain a constant. Another example is power distribution. It was first accomplished in factories with overhead belts being driven by a steam engine. Power distribution continues as a given today, although the belts and the original steam engine are mostly gone. Action was visible in the old factories. As we approach nanotechnology manufacturing action will be nearly invisible.

ALLOWABLE INNOVATION

Commenting on business today, Alan Greenspan has said, "Adapt or lose out." He also stressed in the same talk the need for far better change education and training. Charles Darwin suggested that the tool of successful evolution was adaptation. This is change by modification, or what might be called allowable innovation. Allowable innovation is innovation that reasonably measures the cost of innovation, or an accountable innovation. I think people at large allow for change in that fashion. It is the rare change that shocks and occurs instantaneously, and that may be our misperception?

The cost of innovation, or accountable innovation, can be measured in manufacturing only through clear visibility of process. Changes can and must be made, but with reference to the available supply process, the level of the quality process, customer reaction, and numerous other factors. The lack of visibility leads to a lack of accountability, and any subsequent change in the process proceeds in a context of chaos.

Clearly we must change or adapt, as even a degree of chaos is better than the finality of closing the doors. The question is how do we minimize the risks of change?

DARKNESS VISIBLE

There must be a mission within which the change occurs. The mission consists of a plan for or a vision by which the enterprise goes ahead. The vision must reflect a true view of the realities of the enterprise, and should provide a real-time visibility of the functioning enterprise and its potentiality within the context of the market or markets within which it operates or hopes to operate.

There are several mistakes—stones in the path of successful change—that may trip an enterprise. The first and probably the most dangerous is overdependence on technology at the expense of a planned strategy. The second may be a naïveté that centers on the lack of understanding of the complexity of process integration; parts do not make a product. The third is underestimating the cost of change in its full measure. The fourth is underestimating the need to reeducate all members of the work force and the attendant cost of that effort. The fifth, and possibly the most intractable, is the resistance to a corporate cultural change, the habits of use, and long-term acceptance.

When it comes to change, the greatest risk of all is to take no risk at all.

The reduction of risk is dependent on information that is both pertinent (right area) and timely (right time). This means having visibility, and visibility is dependent on having the proper information from the proper place at the proper time. Risk today is therefore a great spur to increased use of visibility tools (software and hardware) and greatly increased feedback (by electronic communication) of critical information: position, condition, open, closed, hot, cold, etc.

If we are going to survive most risk, we might start by thinking through the steps and the sequence of the steps as a choreographed symphony or dance. When faced with risk (more risk than usual), having a plan is a must and a first priority.

MANAGEABLE RISK

Let us look at risk from a logistics perspective, as in shipping container inspection, a popular idea these days with increased world trade multiplied by ever-increasing terrorism. The idea of 100 percent inspection of shipping containers is at the core of the dream of total port security here and abroad.

There are alternatives, and they are alternatives people will have to get used to sooner or later, according to Stephen E. Flynn, the Jeanne F. Kirkpatrick Senior Fellow in National Security, Council on Foreign Relations. The ubiquitous shipping container that costs only $1,800 to send from China to the United States commands his attention. According to Flynn, this box has caused a transportation revolution and a vulnerability.

However, the container did not catch on right away, as there were all kinds of logistic mismatches between ship, crane, truck, and rail to be figured out. But these issues were figured out and containers are now at the core of international trade. Unfortunately, the supply chains of the world have not seen security as an economic advantage. Security has been seen as a complicated cost. Regardless, the vulnerability is there and must be coped with sensibly.

VULNERABILITY

Flynn (among others) is most worried about the vulnerability of the individual container. The case can be made most cogently by tracing a shipping container from Asian points (the vast majority these days) east by ship to the West Coast (Vancouver, Tacoma, or Seattle), and then east farther to, say, Chicago, where what was assumed to be an innocent shipment of shoes or socks turns out to be a dirty bomb. At each point in the trip there is a degree of vulnerability: while being trucked locally, and then repeatedly at each intermodal transfer of the container.

The question to be asked is at what point was the container compromised? It could be at almost any point, as the security in most cases is lax. Can we find and identify this container out of 200 million containers? Do we shut down the ports—as was done on the West Coast for different reasons a few years ago—when a problem arises? Flynn and others suggest that the intelligent course of action is to be as secure as possible. The private sector, not the government, is ready to do that now, without the further pilot studies that are suggested by governments. Flynn also suggests that we depend on the resiliency of the intermodal transportation system. He advocates letting the intermodal system continue to run even if a bad event occurs. The alternative is to close down, which could lead to possible nationwide or worldwide economic disaster.

Flynn cites the July 2005 London subway bombings as a case in which intelligent reaction to terror kept the systems going. He is convinced that there are ways for our ports to be made more secure using available and already tested techniques at an affordable price. That means going from 1 percent container surveillance up to 99 percent within a reasonable time frame.

A recent U.S. government response is the enactment of the Security and Accountability for Every Port Act. It authorizes the expenditure of $6.7 billion to make our ports secure, with 100 percent radiation inspection of all containers. It should be noted in this context that the baggage on most of our commercial flights has *no* security check whatsoever.

AN AGE OF RISK

Any realistic approach to risk has to recognize that risk cannot be fully eliminated. Any effort to fully conquer risk is bound for failure. The challenge of risk has been a human problem since time immemorial. To do business is to be at risk. To manufacture and sell products is to be at risk—just ask Sony, Ford, and GM recently. To run an airline is to be at risk. To receive containers at ports is to be at risk, as the handlers of bomb-sniffing dogs know well.

Today we are in the Age of Risk. It means that rather than worrying so much about what might happen, we worry about what is happening and why we can't stop it.

We have all kinds of tools for forecasting risk, but when push comes to shove, a single aberrant person or a sudden natural event can throw all the forecasting to the wind. Who would anticipate an animal eating through a power cable? The same dynamic applies in forecasting demand on a manufacturing line. A brand new, unexpected competitor can put the whole business at risk.

RISK METER

The costs involved in any particular risk such as the launch of a new product, the delivery of vital computer parts, or the availability of a particular port for loading have to be weighed against all the other risks of an enterprise. A risk has to be given a priority. Risks must be assigned a place on the risk meter.

For example, the supply chain's vulnerability was deeply at risk when Hurricane Katrina hit New Orleans in 2005. Many have asked why Wal-Mart had a plan in place to deal with this situation and FEMA didn't. (FEMA was just one part of a failed federal response.) As early as 1969, Wal-Mart had already adopted just-in-time strategies (J-I-T) for its supply chain. Just-in-time is a methodology that gets the right goods and materials to the right places at the right time and with strict quality control.

Wal-Mart is a supply chain. Wal-Mart has an excellent vision and execution plan for most forms of supply chain events. It understands supply chain and logistics priorities. Essentially, Wal-Mart *is* its supply chain. After Hurricane Katrina, Wal-Mart restored its stores quickly and stocked them. FEMA, on the other hand, had no plan that it could actually act upon. Being prepared really means being ready to execute your plan.

CREATING PRIORITIES

There is what might be called easy triage that consists of saving or not saving just anybody or anything. Then there is tough triage, where it is a question of either saving your mother or saving your daughter. This is a kind of risk that has no positive solution.

When we turn our attention to port security, it becomes clear that we cannot realistically plan to fully inspect all containers and all bulk cargo. (Containers hold material in steel boxes, while bulk cargo can be in open bins, as in train cars or cars stacked on carriers.) So how do we handle risk in that case? In a medical context, the use of triage calls for saving the one that can be saved regardless of the dramatic nature of the wounds or the time of the person's arrival. The surgeons save those they can and in an order of priority, and reluctantly let the others go. It is practical and intelligent, and, to some, surely seems calloused. One hundred percent inspection of any extended supply chain is a dream.

BEATING RISK

Find the source of the risk and, if possible, beat out the risk. If the risk is coming from a competitor and the competitor is vulnerable, a decision may be made to go outside and do something (e.g., act in a predatory way and eliminate its supply chain) or stay inside and react to the challenge. This is essentially what is done when a company goes through the process of outsourcing. The company must determine whether the job can be better handled outside or if it should improve its inside performance. This is an aggressive way to deal with risk.

Some companies spread risk by utilizing some form of insurance. This had its origins with the Dutch traders who endured long and dangerous yet potentially profitable voyages by ship in the 14th through 17th centuries. By adding a greater number of players, they were able to lower their risk, at least in financial terms. While the sailors might die, the financiers survived. A similar formula exists today in collaboration. More players in serious collaborations come to less risk if the collaboration holds.

Franchise is another clever form of insurance. I give you what you don't have (a plan and execution system for a restaurant) and you give me local management, some funding, and labor. Risk in logistics is to a great extent handled through third-party logistics (3PL) relationships. The 3PLs get paid to take the level of risk agreed upon in the contract or partnership.

Currently, the most vulnerable to risk are the most obvious: shipping containers (because they seem to be vulnerable even though no real damage has been incurred) and airlines. Less obvious are the airfreight pallets that are stored in an aircraft's cargo hold and the bulk cargo that goes in and out of ports daily. A huge bomb could be concealed in a grain shipment.

A CHAIN SMOKER

Let me use an example that occurred at the Port of Seattle. One day at the port two trained security dogs sniffed and did not pass on two containers from Asia. The containers were flagged as bomb risks and set aside. After drilling into the containers, port officials found them to contain rags and clothing for recycling (a common container load). Some of the rags were oil soaked, but there was no bomb present in either container. Because the manifest accompanying these containers was not accurate, the officials could not initially determine which ship had borne the containers or from which port they had come. False information was originally given, but later corrected. Meanwhile, a security circle had been created for hundreds of yards around the containers, which were just a short distance from downtown Seattle. The potential danger was real, though the response was amateurish. The containers full of dirty rags should have been properly labeled, with a manifest to match. The problem's solution should have occurred at the starting gate and not at the final destination.

If one of those containers had held a dirty bomb, an atomic bomb, or just a plain old bomb, the city could have encountered various levels of risk. Security applied after the fact is no security at all.

Meeting risks may call for any number of special considerations; each part, each material, each subassembly, each product has to be handled with different planning, tools, and processes. This is what increases the cost and the complexity of processing. Risks are rarely alike, and in most cases, we need to apply anticipatory planning.

ANTICIPATION IS THE THING

Buckminster Fuller was an advocate of anticipatory design. In his solving exercises, he advocated that his students learn to anticipate a need, a problem, and a complication.

Any intelligent examination will try to create through anticipation a plan, a method, an ace in the hole. Who would have thought that housing would be the result of looking at the expansion of a tetrahedron onto the surface of a sphere from which we get geodesic lines that act as assembly points for a Fuller dome?

Fuller's anticipation looked for the negative spaces. He applied this anticipatory design to many, many versions of his dome. Each time the dome became easier to erect and easier to manufacture. He increased their simplicity and increased their strength while making them faster to erect. He took risk out by anticipation.

REASONABLE FLEXIBILITY

When was the last time you saw someone use a Swiss Army knife? While too little flexibility can lead one to get starchy, stiff, unimaginative, or worse, too much flexibility is no flexibility at all. This means that too many choices lead to an inability to make any choice at all. We can fog over when trying to choose from all the varieties of cheese, breakfast cereal, or yogurt at the supermarket. We as consumers can be overtaxed in our ability to differentiate. Just ask anyone trying to differentiate between the numerous cell phone services.

If we apply this thinking to supply chain risk, we have to become aware that having too many options for containment or control, too many cooks, too many and unsorted emergencies, can be a problem. We can exhaust ourselves not making a decision. We can divide our force when what we need is concentration. We can mistake the trees for the forest and the battle for the war. It takes keen judgment to reduce the options, the flexibility, and the spread.

RISK CALLS FOR A SENSE OF WHOLENESS

The key is to have a sense of the big picture, the gestalt, the overview, the integration of the parts into a meaningful picture, pattern, or solution. Allow me to give an example. At the Guggenheim Museum in New York, a person comes to visit the director, walks up the ramp, and notices that there is an Alexander Calder exhibit being installed. The visitor sees Calder coming down the ramp. Calder asks the visitor if she can help him fix one of his stabiles that got damaged during the transportation. The visitor volunteers and makes adjustments to the stabile as Calder supervises. A guard, observing a stranger making changes to a work of art, races to the rescue and stops the visitor. Calder grabs the guard to disengage him from his tackle. They all roll on the floor until the curator arrives and restores order. Everyone has done his or her job and it all comes out badly. They each are part of a drama that has no central script. The museum must manage the risks of damage, vandalism, and theft. The stakes are high. The artist owns his or her work and aims to restore it to its original form. The visitor merely tries to accommodate the artist. No one has the big picture in mind. The consequence is a struggle.

RADIATING BROCCOLI?

There is no place that has gotten more attention in regard to security risks than container ports, and the big picture is essential.

These ports vie with airports as the core of our perception of security risks. Recently at the Port of Rotterdam, a container came in and set off the security alarms that were sensitive to radiation. The security department reacted swiftly, concerned that the container might house a dirty bomb. In fact, it contained broccoli in its handpicked form, which naturally contains a low level of radiation. A full container of it was sufficient to bring out the guard.

For the railroads, big pictures are hard to come by. Not many years ago, the railroads thought they were in the train business, until they were told they were in the transportation business. What business do you think you are in? If companies or industries persist in misinterpreting what they are, they are at risk. Knowing what you are becomes the first order of business.

GOING DYSTELEOLOGICAL

Now the word *dysteleology* is a mouthful, but its parts are all Greek. "Dys" means hard, difficult, or bad; "teleo" means goal, end, or purpose; and "logos" means the study of. The parts together may thereby mean the study of difficult ends, or the study of bad goals or worst scenarios. The study of the worst scenario is of a very different order than the common kind of crisis management or disaster relief used after meltdown, flood, hurricane, or earthquake. The emphasis in these cases is on what we do *after* the worst happens.

What I am suggesting is studying what we can do to identify the worst scenarios, and then determine what might be done to correct the condition such a calamity may inflict, before, during, and after the event strikes. Instead of being reactive, I am advocating that we be predictive and proactive.

This is a very serious matter, and recent U.S. history is fraught with inadequacy. We have failed to see the worst possibilities in the use of planes as weapons. We have failed to see a building itself as an unstable bomb in the making. We have failed in not being able to see a truck as a weapons delivery system.

We failed historically to see poorly designed steel plates, or light plates, or aluminum plates (used to construct the *Titanic*, *HMS Hood*, and battleships used in the Falklands Islands war) as weaknesses that can destroy a ship. We still don't understand suicide attacks or their consequences. We failed to see the U.S. mail as a means of distributing anthrax, even though other nasty devices had been distributed this way for years. Before 9/11, we did not see the supply chain and transportation as targets.

There are dozens of such failures in the larger world, and even in the more local logistics or business world. For instance, a company may fail to understand the consequences of getting the wrong thing to the wrong place at the wrong time. Or it might fail to see the consequences of having either no inventory or endless inventory. An excess of inventory or inventory held too long is a cost and a tax cost.

Studying the worst scenario means making the examination of the worst circumstances a regular methodology.

SUMMING UP: RISK AND ADAPTATION

Risk has changed for us. The volume has turned up. Information flows not just faster but in ever greater quantities. Risk flows in ever-increasing quantities. We are either planning or anticipating risk, or we are suffering its consequences. There is no such thing as full security from risk, but having a reasonable perspective on it will mean passing on to your customer a sense of security to the extent that it is possible.

Chapter

3

REALITY CRUNCH: OUR PERCEPTIONS AND REACTIONS

UNDERSTANDING REALITY IN A CRUNCH!

The appropriateness of behavior and decision making is critical when operating in the real world (unlike in a video game or fantasy movie). It does not help to dust the deck chairs as the *Titanic* is sinking. It does not really help to dredge the bottom of a harbor when the ships are too big to pass under critical bridges that dominate the path of those ships. It does not help to widen roads that don't have existing traffic.

Robert Ballard, the great underwater adventurer, discovered that, much to his embarrassment, it was not necessary to go down in a submersible to view life at the bottom of the sea. Why deep-sea dive when a robot can do it? He found this out accidentally when he took a biologist to look at life around deep-sea smokers. The biologist did not look at the creatures through the portholes, but by observing them on a TV within the submersible. Why subject yourself to work that is not necessary when a robot can actually do it better, longer, cheaper? In this case, reality was on the screen and not in the water.

Tracking goods in a logistics process can be done on a screen as well through the use of sensors, bar codes, or RFID technology. Being physically present is often not necessary in routine processes.

MISUNDERSTANDINGS

In the 1970s, the United States Postal Service resisted the push toward automation, citing concerns about the loss of jobs. This lack of vision brought it close to becoming completely obsolete. FedEx, DHL, and UPS were quick to pick up the ball the USPS has dropped. Prior to these events, the public did not utilize commercial carriers nearly as much as they do today. The U.S. Post Office is now working far better, and oddly, has developed partnerships with some of the commercial carriers.

CEOs of big companies, as well, can have lapses in their understanding of reality. Ken Olson at Digital, and his total misunderstanding of the advent and the importance of the personal computer, is an example of the awful decision making that in many ways led to the collapse of his great company. The company instead held to its minicomputer business and missed out on a chance to be a significant player in the personal computer revolution.

"LOOK FOR THE EMPTIES" OR THE NAPKINS

If you want to spot a supply chain, in the words of Bob Ballard, "Look for the empties"; that's how he found the remains of the *Titanic* and many other underwater relics. Things leave a trail. Ships leave a wake; trucks leave tracks; bills of lading show up on the manifest. A sinking ship does not drop to the bottom of the ocean like a rock. It first sheds its goods, and in a specific order. It is the nature of a sinking ship to act this way. Ballard used this real and traceable fact as his search mechanism. This means using the process of an event like the sinking to find the ship. It's a kind of reverse engineering.

In business, there is the case of an economist who looked for a means to gauge the economy. He came up with a trail: the number of napkins from good restaurants in New York that were being laundered. He traced back from the laundry the scale of increase, or decrease, and found that it matched earlier rises and falls in the economy. Good eating, good economy. The trail is what the supply chain is all about in many ways. No trail, no track—and lots of misinformation.

Then there was the case of the store-location genius. Years ago, he determined that the best place to put a store was where there was the most constant traffic of people. Where the people are, the store should be. This is retailing 101—and 102. The ignorance of this insight in retailing is hideous waste.

Another case in point is the automobile designer's crash test. The designer can see after examining a crashed vehicle the nature of its collapse, denting, and crushing. The accident's effects on the car's metal and plastic leave a trail. By reverse engineering, designers can make the car safer in the event of an accident.

Finally, bridge designers learned from the destruction of the Tacoma Bridge that wind factors could bring a bridge down. They then started redesigning bridges to be aerodynamically sound. In each of these cases, demand regulates supply. In each case, reality intrudes upon the scene or redirects the action.

CHALLENGING STRENGTH

Challenging the Japanese on automotive quality, for instance, is to go after their strength. It is a tough proposition and one hard to accomplish. Beating them in design and marketing may be far easier but, in the long run, not sustaining. Therefore, possibly the best strategy is to aim for quality over a period of years, and not just on one model. The goal has to be persistent winning.

Another way is to look for the weakest link in a chain. For the Japanese, this weakness may be a high degree of innovation. For instance, Japanese automakers went overboard in offering cars with endless options, and this both increased costs and made the choice for customers too difficult. After seeing consumer reactions, they refined this cornucopia of offering.

TRACING

An unsealed package has telltale traces. Packages of food, medicine, and electronics parts are now created to show when having been opened (or tampered with). The paper, the plastic, the seal can't be reassembled without enormous effort. To do so would require the original packing equipment. While this can be inconvenient to the user, it is a great protection.

Another example might be the coding of item-level RFID products. The product can be traced; this is a convenience for the retailer but a possible invasion of privacy for the buyer. Security from theft no longer requires an individual to examine the product to determine if it was removed illicitly; rather the item's tag alerts the store that an item is leaving that has not been processed by the checkout. Instead of a trail or telltale sign, the RFID inlay communicates condition without a trail or an inspection. The item speaks for itself.

LOOK FOR THE BREAKDOWNS

We don't know the reality of a process until it breaks down. In fact, most people don't have the slightest idea how machines work until they either try to repair them or have to pay big money to have someone else repair them. The same is true for processes. Until a computer network breaks down, the knowledge of that network can often be rather superficial.

When artificial intelligence (AI) came into being, one of its profitable discoveries was expert systems. An expert system is one that can mimic or match an expert. The system designers found out how an expert worked by trial and error questioning and watching. If the expert was an expert in steam boilers, they watched, recorded, and studied each action and each sequence in whatever circumstances the process took. They were often amazed to find out how people (experts) actually cared for and repaired their machines. Engineers listened to the machines, they judged the temperature by their own cheeks, and they talked to the machine the way some people talk to flowers. The designers found that in using machines or controlling mechanisms, logic was often subservient to remembered procedures or routines, even if those routines weren't necessarily productive—tapping the boiler, kicking a stanchion, oiling again what no longer needs to be oiled. Yet they would find gold as some seemingly odd procedures bore fruit. They had adapted their own work habits to the perceived need of the machine or process. Automation can mimic some of these responses and, in time, probably successfully, but we may not be there yet.

ADAPTIVE BEHAVIOR

Waiting brings out all kinds of activity that can be redundant, productive, or simply let off steam. Complex adaptive behavior thrives on anticipation. The modern company would do well to create teams rather than a pyramid of management. Teams are interactive by their nature. Watch a baseball team adjust to a heavy left-handed hitter. This is adaptive response of a most complex order. The team changes positions to cope with the hitter, and each team member adjusts to the others' responses. The team acts as one organism.

Adaptive response to change can give real-time response to actual conditions and trends, rather than assumptions based on abstract speculation. This is a response based on reality rather than an assumption about reality.

In logistics, pickup and delivery can act like an intelligent thermostat in a home, like a proximity sensor in a robot, like a directive sensor in a navigation system. Adaptive change can make for flexible response and control. Adaptive change can smooth the flow of the business processes. There is no time in business more critical than the time of launch into a fresh new market.

FIRST MOVES

The first moves in business (launching a new product, taking on the big competition, outsourcing, new suppliers, and the procurement tree) set off a whole flood of consequences. There are no isolated actions in business. There is an organic connection even between processes that may appear to be separate. Eventually all processes affect all other processes.

As an example, let's look at recycling. It really is reverse manufacturing, but people don't see it that way. Recycling starts with planning the product or the process. In order to successfully recycle, the capability for recycling has to be built in. The system of logistics for the recycling process should be anticipated as well. The reality of a product is its full life cycle, and not just the time during which it is being used. People too often see recycling as a burden and not as part of the cycle. The movement of goods to manufacturing and the movement of the product through the store to the consumer, both leave a trail of paper, cardboard, and packaging that must also in time be recycled.

REMOVING THE MIDDLE

The supply chain lends itself to reduction. The middleman in the supply chain may be removed altogether by a through service from a manufacturer to a buyer. Processes in the logistics of the supply chain can be removed by intelligent design and planning. For instance, the storage of goods requires unloading, sorting, and storing, and later more sorting and possibly packaging and transport. If the supply chain is sufficiently tuned, the storage may be altogether unneeded. Storage can be the result of mistaken capacity planning, overzealous ordering, bad seasonal judgment, or poor market interpretation.

THE QUESTION OF TECHNOLOGY

Although we may find it hard to believe, people had technology before computers were invented. They called it other things, most often referring to an object such as steam engine or other machine. In its modern form, "technology" has come to mean almost everything, but in engineering terms, it refers to an applied system in fields such as communication technology, nuclear technology, or robotics technology. A technology becomes, therefore, an assemblage of tools, techniques, machines, and processes. A technology is not a thing so much as a connection of things acting toward some end.

We date ourselves by the outdated products of technology, whether they are telephones, TVs, cars, weapons, or clothes such as shirts with stiff collars, buttoned sweaters, and spats.

Technologies as applied can tend to overpower, as in the case of personal computer technology in the United States in the period from 1980 to 2000, or dot-com technology in the latter part of the 20th century and the first part of this century. They overpowered in that they were not merely replacements, nor simple in their focus, but were new in what they offered and in the sheer breadth of their application.

Technology does not necessarily get us closer to reality or to the solutions that might make life better. It often promises to improve an activity, enlarge a world, make a process cheaper, but none of these promises should go unexamined.

SUMMING UP: REALITY IN PERSPECTIVE

We may take comfort in saying to ourselves that reality and fantasy can be mixed, and that it is not serious when they are, but the only businesses that run on pure fantasy are professional wrestling, Hollywood, Disney, and the like. Even in logistics, reality can be hard to pin down; a grasp of the realities of business, economics, the supply chain, and the market is essential.

Chapter 4

LEONARDO FLUNKED LATIN: INNOVATING AND INVENTING

You can't force-feed innovation. It leads at best to regurgitation. There is a place in the back of the eye referred to as the blind spot because it does not recognize light. When you need to look critically at something, you want to avoid the blind spot—to ensure nothing obscures your vision. It is so with innovation; we need to look slightly to the edge, to the places beyond the obvious. It is there that we shall find the key to successful supply chain business practice and the means to hold on to our customers.

We need to question critically anyone who comes up with an innovation tool, an innovation kit, an innovation "snake oil." Can there really be an innovation strategy? If there is an innovation strategy in place, what has it innovated?

INNOVATION DOES NOT EXIST IN A VACUUM

Innovation may partake of the Universal Unconscious that was offered to the world by psychologist Carl Jung. There are dragons in all world cultures, according to some. The fact of fictional shared dragons does not prove Jung's theory. If we share unconsciously, we don't seem to have enough evidence to confirm the sharing.

But ideas percolate. Any student of the history of technology will find countless examples of innovations and inventions that appear to have been discovered or conceived at the same time: the bar code, the TV, the computer, the airplane. Some of these claims are questionable, but others, such as the computer, appear solid.

People sitting around in a room dreaming up ideas is not innovating. In the ordinary course of life, innovating does not occur by command. For instance, being a vice president of innovation means essentially nothing. It is not an assignment and therefore innovating is not done like homework. Innovating is not practicing, as in piano lessons. Innovating may be more like waiting or paying attention. Innovating may be more passive than active. This has to be very frustrating for the captains of industry; innovating can't be bought until after the fact.

LEONARDO FLUNKED LATIN

Leonardo da Vinci did not have a classical Latin education. He never really got the language down. So he missed, to a great extent, the "wisdom" of the authoritative fathers. Instead he looked at nature—not at someone's speculations (and more speculations built on more speculations). Da Vinci innovated based on his observations of real things, such as observing a flayed cadaver for its actual muscle structure, or noting the configuration of a plant as it grows and as it is really is put together—vein, leaf, and stem.

The 17th-century astronomer and thinker Johannes Kepler had a dream. After trying to work out the nature of planetary motion from the historic premise of circular orbits, he found himself getting nowhere. He had better planetary motion data than anyone had up to his time, but he could not make the orbits fit into circular forms. It is claimed that in a dream, or coming out of a dream, he realized that the planets moved not in circles, as would appear to the average person, but in elliptical arcs that couldn't be seen by the naked eye or sensed over time. Only elliptical orbits would explain the position of the planets as observed. The abstraction of ancient and relied-upon lore had sent him in the wrong direction.

Thomas Edison did not have a corner on invention or innovation. He had a corner on some very bright staff members and a dedication to continuous and arduous work. He had powerful friends and a rather large ego. He and his associates are often set up as the paragons of innovation—and their record is impressive. Edison is given credit for the light bulb, but there were a host of others at the time going in a similar direction. Did he win because he had a better bulb, or because he was well positioned, having already invented and been given claim to his inventions and the innovations of existing inventions? It may have been not so much Edison's own inspiration, as testing under the smart eye of his aide and educated scientist, Charles Steinmetz.

Alan Turing, a mathematician and clearly a creative man, worked for the British during World War II, attempting to break the German code. Turing invented a machine that had almost all the characteristics of the computer. Its purpose was to process code combinations accurately, and faster than many people. It succeeded. Turing's other work included the Turing test, which evaluates a machine's ability to carry on a humanlike conversation. His work was a precursor to the development of the computer and artificial intelligence.

SOME COMPANIES HAVE IMAGINATION

The innovation of one truck for each delivery zone may have occurred to the United States Postal Service before it occurred to Jim Casey, the founder of UPS. It was an essential connection in order to make a delivery system or business successful. It is hard to know who came up with the idea of tracking items from their origin and tracking them repeatedly. It was surely associated with the advent of the application of bar code: label it, scan it, and know where and what it is. FedEx may have invented or innovated the concept and, far harder, the practice of next-day delivery; however, an airfreight system had to be in place before this process was possible.

Toyota should be given credit for the full-blown idea of one-off manufacturing. Mass production of a single item seems so absurd except when customers make it profitable. Through the use of selective software, a car can be assembled within a production line as if it were a single production. It is customized without modifying the factory as a whole, and thus we have a "one-off," because the cars before and after the customized vehicle are not customized to the same specifications. It sets off a whole series of required logistics moves throughout the supply chain. These may be big concepts such as just-in-time (J-I-T), or little concepts such as the use of a "U" configuration at a manufacturing work station: the worker moves in a U-shaped work space, which has proved to be, as in kitchens, the most effective means of work. This concept works in manufacturing and in warehousing and logistics generally. Another case in point: The concept of transport associated to cost may well have been an adjunct to the implementation of intermodal transport advantage. It would mean a mandate to carry freight upon the mode that provides the greatest savings. The idea is to provide a flow that reduces waste, as in the overuse of trucks for long-haul transport. Each step as in a U-shaped workspace is measured for its efficiency.

TECHNIQUES FOR INNOVATION

When a process is examined in reverse, as in a film run backward, many connections can reveal themselves that we might not otherwise notice. It is the same with stop action and slow forward. The sports industry has used these devices for years, benefiting from the ability to revisit and reexamine their actions.

The same is true in the manufacturing process. The use in logistics in this arena has been marginal, although the trucking industry has, according to the American Trucking Association (ATA), looked at the correlations between driver behavior and fuel consumption and the efficiency of the engine's operation. If we see a truck loaded in a film run backward, what will we see? If we look closely, we may see that the truck bed and the loading dock are poorly aligned, or that the use of a forklift actually impedes loading because it requires a pallet that raises the load so it hits the top of the trailer. We are surprised by what we see using a fresh perspective; that is, we are seeing innovatively.

REVERSE ENGINEERING

The practice of reverse engineering is a tried and true methodology in engineering. It simply means to work the process backward. This requires going from result back to cause, from finished product back to parts, from finished design back to elements, from the delivery back to the point of origin. What are the parts? What are the events? Can some elements be removed? Can some parts be miniaturized? Can some processes be minimized? Can some parts or processes be made at a lower cost? Might the act of trying to make them cheaper lead to better designed parts and better articulated processes? Is the value of the product or process apparent, and does it need to be? The means of accomplishing these feats can occur by breaking down the product or process and examining each individual element, or, in the other direction, by looking at the whole product or the whole process and determining if it reflects what has gone into it.

THE RELATIONSHIP OF DEMAND AND AVAILABILITY

Many products that were developed and used in great quantity are no longer available. There are many reasons for this: aerosol cans caused environmental damage, the Edsel was an awful concept and design, and the Airflow Chrysler was ahead of its time. The Edsel was shocking because of its radical front-end design (though its function was standard Ford), while the Airflow Chrysler was too many steps forward in design and was not on the buying public's radar screen.

This is also evident with delivery services that once were standard but are now not as readily available, such as home delivery of milk and ice, or knife and scissor sharpening. But new services have arisen to meet new demands, such as Fresh Direct—a company that delivers groceries that are ordered online. This delivery model necessitates a uniquely efficient supply chain because the food must be fresh as delivered, the food varies in its longevity, and both customer and retailer are reliant on their Internet connections.

NEXT STEPS IN INNOVATION

Innovation takes place in steps. Aircraft were first pushed by propellers placed in the back, then they were pulled by propellers in the front, and now they are propelled by jets. The first computers were the size of a basketball court with very slow action, yet today they can fit in the palm of your hand and connect you to the world in an instant. When we look at a product, we must evaluate whether it is the finished product or service, or only a step in the process.

However, we know we have gone one too far when things begin to unhinge, when too many unnecessary features eclipse the core feature. A fountain pen that is also a pimento remover or eyelash trimmer is not going to be a big seller at The Sharper Image. A practical innovation will not negate one function over another, or to put the two out of phase; that is, it is not useful for the eraser to outlast the lead in the pencil.

Changes in technology, such as the 200-gigabyte laptop and the new microchip that is the size of grain of rice, have to be harbingers of the future. We seem to be moving toward recording everything, tagging everything with RFID, tracking everything, and being in constant communication at all times. New robots know where they are. Robots that work in warehouses not only know where they are; large numbers of them can move in a warehouse space, avoid each other, and move quite expeditiously.

Let's look at innovation in the areas of manufacturing, commercial carriers, retail distribution, and business process.

MANUFACTURING INNOVATES

Manufacturing has gone through a number of innovative steps as it has moved from mass manufacture to manufacture for one, or from made-to-stock to made-to-order. Correspondingly, there has been a movement from satisfying the factory manager to satisfying the customer. It has required integration of information from machines, processes, and people. The difference between made-to-order and made-to-stock is day and night. Made-to-stock means warehouses and inventory. Made-to-order means meeting real-time demand as it drives manufacturing. It has made manufacturers evolve from trying to add quality to a transformation or process at the end to implementing quality at the beginning.

The manufacturer has seen a transformation in the way parts are delivered within manufacturing. Today, they are often "kitted," as in the assembly of a Dell computer. This means the parts necessary for the one-off Dell computer arrive at the assembly station in a box (a kit) with all the parts necessary for that assembly.

Manufacturers have found new ways to design products for manufacturing while taking into consideration the challenge of their delivery to the ultimate customer. This is a prime feature of IKEA and leads to packaging with no empty space. The products are assembled by consumers who have brought them home from the store by their own conveyances. Consumers are co-opted into being part of IKEA's supply chain.

COMMERCIAL CARRIERS INNOVATE

Innovation in trucking comes at all levels. Simply regulating tire pressure can lead to saving fuel: underinflated tires use more fuel. Truckloads without pallets are a simple innovation, but one that's only rarely implemented. The pallets take up a large amount of space and are not value added; rather, they cost money to transport.

The meeting of wireless communication and transportation management systems software has been especially beneficial. Fleets of trucks and now trains on rail can be managed and have their routes or schedules changed while they are en route. These are not genius breakthroughs; rather, they are pragmatic, successful trends. It is now possible for carriers to use wireless technology to phase their traffic on highways and avoid congested conditions.

In airfreight, plane flight paths can be now be reduced electronically. Engine design innovation means that planes can be made to go farther on the same amount of fuel. Creating stretch versions of the planes has provided increased interior space with a minimal increase in fuel use. Some changes that are very simple pay off big time, such as stretch planes, while others, such as improved blade design on jets, are the result of thousands of hours of design and engineering time.

The concept of stretching has been applied nowhere more fully than in containerships. They get longer by the minute, as do the containers they carry, which started out at 20 feet and now are 53 feet long. A 20-footer is nearly as difficult to handle at a port as a 53-footer. The limit for containers is constrained by trucks and their handling in city traffic. Rail carriers can handle 53-footers on a single level or as stacking containers. This neat trick is a simple but profitable example of innovation. The containers may be stacked on the trains because they have their own high path right of way, while trucks do not. That is one advantage rail can take to the bank.

RETAIL DISTRIBUTION INNOVATES

Retail establishments have their own special ways of innovating. Some start with virtual warehouses or leased warehouses. This means either giving a third-party provider the warehousing function, or utilizing a warehouse someone else puts up, and possibly manages, with a lease deal. In terms of their large-scale applications these techniques are relatively new. Retailers that work closely with third-party logistics providers may decrease their delivery costs by intermodal transfers or through the technique of merge in transit, or cross docking. RFID carton and pallet tagging has become an innovative way to accomplish J-I-T delivery. Merge in transit is a transportation technique that provides simultaneous delivery of shipments from different origin points; once completed, the shipment can be tracked using one ID number. Cross docking is a means by which a truck loaded with goods transfers those goods directly (or almost) to another truck inside a distribution center with the opportunity to do sorting of goods and provide a new specific delivery destination.

BUSINESS PROCESSING INNOVATES

Businesses have evolved from clipboards to relational databases and accompanying handheld or portable computing devices. These improvements have, in addition, moved them from relational databases to data warehouses, from unaccountable business to compliance, and now to business intelligence tools and wireless data access. It has meant using such techniques as text analysis to get rid of confused information. Data systems need to be robust and flexible in order to handle information from so many sources. The supply chain and logistics can be messy. Any system should have enough robustness to deal with variability, and we should too. Clutter is not necessarily a drawback. Clutter provides an opportunity to unclutter. A mess is an opportunity to bring about order.

It is the nature of innovation to upset the logistics carts and the supply chain theories. The Japanese like neatness and have made it into a manufacturing "science." It can work for them in processing of manufactured goods, but it does not necessarily work as a better means of idea generation, nor is it a direct means to information clarity.

BACK DOOR INNOVATION

Short cuts can lead to invention and innovation. Isaac Asimov wanted a short way to say the "study of robots" and coined the word *robotics*. John Diebold, the father of modern information technology, found the word *automatization* too difficult to spell, and used the word *automation* instead.

Much of pedagogical advice runs to tried and "true" methods; for instance, *focus*. If we focus too soon we do not understand context. If we focus too late we may miss the action. Or consider *concentrate*. If we concentrate, we again rule out the perimeter. If we concentrate, we freeze the roaming and the pickups from the subconscious. Or *analyze it*. Parsing may make clear the structure of the sentence but it does not make the sentence any better or worse. Seeing the parts may miss the gestalt of the whole. I think many of us miss both the parts and the whole.

SUMMING UP: INNOVATING

Innovation most certainly is not beyond being organized, but it can't be nailed down all too directly. A carpenter would probably describe it as a towing job (nailing at an angle as the nail is driven). It is little wonder that companies such as Microsoft maintain a campus-like atmosphere where people's offices seem more like dorm rooms. We have to come at innovation obliquely. Today, it involves innovation of processes as much as innovation of things. This modification is an indication of the trend of modern times. Innovation can occur in multiple places simultaneously, as we are not alone. It can't be planned for or ordered. Innovation may come about through a dream, through egotistical moxie, through a mix of unlike things or people, and through intelligent anticipation. It may be a function of reversing a process, or it may follow a series of steps. Innovation by people is a wonder to behold, and a catalyst for businesses and their supply chains.

Chapter

5

FIVE-MINUTE PLAN: ENHANCING BUSINESS PROCESSES

Let's talk about enhancing. Basically it means improving on a process or product or system, taking the existing and moving it forward—profitably and intelligently if possible—while meeting demand from the system successfully.

ENHANCING CONTROL

Processes are enhanced when they have controls built in, and active, all through the business cycle. Centralized control leads to the manufacturing of only left-footed shoes. Remote or distributed control reinforces reengineering as the control, and the knowledge comes from the process itself and not from an abstraction up the line or up the corporate ladder.

Distributed control got its impetus from the need to coordinate manufacturing, commerce, and retailing as the computer and communications systems made a digital and a Web-based world possible. Isolation by trade or by department or by division might work in a push economy, but it did not come close to working in a pull economy. A push economy is one that manufactures and then finds a buyer (hopefully). A pull economy is based on the specific demands of consumers and manufacturers accordingly. Push is production oriented, while pull is market directed. Tracking capacity and inventory became the core problem. Managers and their employees had to know what the business had, where it was, in what quantity, and of what quality. Remote and distributed control is in its ascendancy.

ENHANCING QUALITY CONTROL

We can enhance products and processes through keeping track of their quality control. This applies to a process such as delivery of packages, to the handling of shipping containers, and to monitoring the quality of parts through the manufacturing cycle or the assembly process. Quality, like security, is best when focused on at the very beginning or initiation of an action. Quality is planned into the process, rather than being discovered after, or not at all. That is to say, quality is designed and not created through final inspection.

What does it mean to improve or increase the speed or quality of production by better process understanding? How do we tune the system? A simple solution for regulating speed in a steam engine in the old days was a ball governor. Processes in manufacturing, logistics, and retailing are not that simple today.

It is probably for that reason that Michael Hammer and James Champy researched and wrote *Reengineering the Corporation,* the classic text on this subject and still a valuable read. We may enhance a company or enterprise or its processes by reengineering it in the ways recommended by its promulgators. This often entails getting closer to the process and trusting knowledge that is close to the process. It is hard to argue with intimate process knowledge. The publication of their book in 1993 matches the enthusiastic blossoming of interest in the supply chain and the advent of the Supply Chain Council.

SCOR IS BORN

The Supply Chain Council's supply-chain operations reference (SCOR) model of the supply chain made it clear that connection and sharing of information would be vital in the process of planning, sourcing, making, distributing, and returning. The SCOR model was a child of the early 1990s and was created to help companies get an overall means of defining, analyzing, and evaluating their supply chains, from the supplier's supplier through to the ultimate customer. It means looking at the supply and demand processes of a company in detail—event by event, process by process. Tools that were once restricted to manufacturing in manufacturing resource planning (MRP) grew out of manufacturing capacity planning as it was needed to govern the quantity and types of resources. Later, enterprise resource planning (ERP) widened the scope to include front office and back office requirements of a company in relation to manufacturing, and then to the supply chain. Programs had to be extended to the whole business and its suppliers and customers. This meant high visibility distributed control of tasks and relationships with supply partners and outlets, ranging from warehouses and distribution centers to wholesalers, retailers, customers, and the customers' customers. It also meant having a return of information and goods system in place. Reverse logistics was born out of this effort, as were new customer feedback mechanisms from marketing, sales, and those managing product life cycles.

DISTRIBUTING CONTROL

A distributed control model based on shared and visible information of markets is more clear-eyed than a centralized control model that operates off abstract plans. The move has been toward giving line managers, supervisors, and individual workers more control. However, this control is regulated by a shared database of information. Delivery truck drivers today spend as much time entering and downloading data from their handheld computers as they do driving or delivering.

There is already a trend toward operator-centric manufacturing and shipping, as with distribution center workers who are connected to a central database, and this means that the goods they supervise are connected too.

Reengineering and focus on the supply chain has essentially revolutionized the processes of business, and workers' relationships to each other and to their jobs.

FIVE-MINUTE PLAN

Despite a good five-year plan, it may behoove us to consider an era of the five-minute plan. A change in the information flow of one function in a digital world can change all information flows and all plans. A change in the material flow of one function changes all material functions and subsequent plans. The only way of dealing with these changes is through greater visibility of process and the distribution of the response to the change. A package today can be changed as to timing and other factors in process. That is the nature of an adaptive system.

A football quarterback is responsible for a plan as close to real time as possible; for him it may be more like a one-second plan. An adaptive response to change means a real-time reaction to actual conditions and trends rather than assumptions based on abstract speculation (or plan). It can translate into a pass rather than a run.

In the world of logistics, pickup and delivery will act like an intelligent thermostat in a home or a directive sensor in a navigation system. Adaptive change can make for flexible response and control. Adaptive change can smooth the flow of the business processes and can generally enhance performance.

UNDERSTANDING CONTEXT

The visibility of a process has to have a context. For instance, the operating efficiency of a single truck or crane has to be looked at in respect to many trucks or a fleet and many cranes and within the context suggested. Operating conditions affect results, as we all know. A truck in the rain or in mountainous terrain is not the same context as a desert. Any test of performance of a truck, as the American Trucking Association can tell you, needs visibility and recording over time. Testing an engine, for instance, on a test platform is not testing an engine on US 495. The method of tracking performance must be judged against other methods of tracking. We have to know what we are looking for in order for us to see well.

THE CRITICAL FACTOR

There are many issues on the radar screen for supply chain managers. The ones that are most important, according to a 2006 report by the Aberdeen Group, are not necessarily those that would first come to mind. The report reflected responses from over 150 enterprises, and suggests that the primary concern of companies is the lack of critical supply chain process visibility, due to their processes being manually, and not automatically, driven. Visibility is a key to business process enhancement. Without process visibility, decisions are made blindly or by the unreliable "seat of the pants" method. Visibility provides the metrics of actual happenings against which improved use of resources can be established.

Fifty-one percent of the respondents in this study chose this as one of their top three concerns. The second most important concern was the uncoordinated multitier supply chain process that leads to an imbalance between supply and demand. Some of the items that respondents would like to have visible, according to the report, included: having order acknowledgment match the purchase order, a view of projected production plans, the visibility that an advanced shipment notice was created, customs clearance, and an available record of in-transit status events at shipment level. In addition, there is a need to know about the raw material arrival at supplier, the supplier's production process events, the advance shipment notice matching the purchase order (a critical security issue), the carrier's pickup of goods, in-transit status events at order line level, and an electronic proof of delivery.

ENHANCING BY REMOVAL

Just as seeing more and better is critical, so process reduction can be a benefit. Removing redundancy is an old reliable form of enhancement (to the bottom line) as in having two batteries rather than four or one disk drive rather than two. It can, of course, be a risky move to reduce in this way because redundancy can also be seen as backup or security.

Removal of waste is a case of simply not letting in error that produces waste. The enhancement comes in the form of reduced costs and a higher level of quality. Removal of waste is a big issue in trucking, for instance, as drivers tend to idle when stopped, rather than shutting off their engines. The fuel wasted is in the millions of gallons in U.S. trucking alone.

The enhancing of a process by removing waste is an effort that goes beyond mere clarity or neatness. Waste can be energy draining, distracting. It is costly, as in taxable warehouse goods. Waste is material or information that is not pertinent to the process at hand and is better removed.

The removal of the extraneous is a Japanese way of enhancing. They practice it in their offering of food, in their packaging, and in their design of motors and cars. Their concept of just-in-time is not just timely delivery. It is the removal of all events, materials, and processes that do not contribute to the essential.

The modern engineer may enhance through the removal of motion. This is nowhere more evident than in the engineering evolution of music players. Tape recorders were essentially spinning motors with tape between and a reading head. Motion, motion, motion; now we have players without any moving parts. Much of modern technology is evolving away from motion to electronic tools that do the same work without the spin. Out with the gears and axles and in with the chips.

When all the waste has been taken out of a process, we should either stick with the process or throw it out and start again if you no longer need the process at all.

CORE INCOMPETENCE

If we are after a unique form of enhancing, we might well look at core incompetence. Core incompetence is essentially that which a company does least well; this might be cost control, product development, assembly design, or materials resourcing. Core competence, on the other hand, is what you assume that you are able to do best; for example, capacity planning, warehousing management, or shipping. Find the error and move ahead. If a company finds its core incompetence, can it reasonably expect to discover by reduction what its core competence is? If all the stuff of less consequence is set aside, what remains? If the process being used is reengineering, then we can expect, if nothing else, fewer people. Redundancy, red tape, and too many levels of management go out the window.

To understand and enhance process, you must know what a process really is. A process is as much a set of interacting responsibilities as it is the interacting of things. A process is in fact a combination of both these factors. Enhancing comes through collaboration, cooperation, and partnering as well as through technology. A process can be a very messy operation: There is as much left over in a process as there is left out.

Enhancing supply chain and logistics performance can be taken on as a positive or negative act, or adding or removing elements, parts, processes. It may best be an activity that spreads the control of process, as in distributed control. Enhancing means placing quality at the beginning of process, and gaining understanding, through analysis such as the SCOR model that reveals what you are really doing. Enhancing the supply chain means, to a great extent, improving visibility while simultaneously removing waste or incompetent and redundant performance.

Visibility is a key, particularly when all the redundancies in a process have been removed. After the scope is directed and the lens is focused, we find what we need to look for and can follow whatever action the information within the view directs us to or warns us about. As any astronomer or ship captain can tell you, seeing is a complex art; and enhanced vision, as any good artist will remind us, is an art form and not a science.

SUMMING UP: ENHANCING

The act of enhancing shares with innovation an element of mystery. It isn't easily put in a box. Enhancing is a by-product of the nature of the control of a product or process. This can involve the design of the process or product, its manufacture, its execution, its distribution, or communication. Today's processes are evolving to remote and distributed control. Today's products are following the same trend as they can act remotely and can have shared control, as in Internet software applications or simply the sharing of pictures that can be downloaded, redesigned, and sent by email. As often as enhancing may be done by addition, it may be matched by reduction. Enhancing is to a great extent practiced well only when a process is fully visible. This has to be coordinated intelligently when operations are spread out geographically, and where control is shared.

Think of the Mars Rover and its control by the staff of Honeybee Robotics. The process on the ground (in New York) and the process on Mars have been designed to allow for coordinated actions. Improvement of performance takes many minds, many remote actions, and the response (delayed by distance) of the Rover. The mission is a fleet of two, and yet has all the complications of Yellow Transportation's management of hundreds of trucks on the road with the same or similar considerations. If you want to improve quality, learn to recognize it first and then design it in, rather than trying to find it later.

The control of a product (package) is possible when we are at or alongside the product and its actions as, for instance, machine tenders or truck delivery drivers. Control is also possible at a distance, remotely, when the action of the process is made highly visible by new communication software and hardware. Visibility is a major means of enhancement in the new worlds of logistics and the supply chain.

Chapter 6

DEUS EX MACHINA: THE GROWTH OF AUTOMATION

A machine has the characteristics of being something that is self-acting. It is in turn the origin of computing, robotics, and automation—a process governed by a set of algorithms is the core of computing. It is the core of software. When we use software, we are taking advantage of a long line of efforts to program the right algorithms at the right time and in the right place.

AUTOMATING

By automation, we mean a method of "thinking" or practicing that induces self-acting behavior on the part of tools, machines, and systems. This behavior does not assume that these processes or objects have intention or will. This stored and self-acting behavior translates into remote control of tools, machines, and system processes that were heretofore more intimate to human activity. It is a question of, wherever possible, making things and data automatic but intelligent with the use of algorithms, repeat sequences, and memory. If the procedure being automated needs correction, this may be accomplished by built-in feedback mechanisms or by reprogramming. This may seem simple, but it took humankind several thousands of years to gain the insights necessary to pull off this set of feats. Feedback is the essential glue that connects action and reaction. It requires that we see things and events in relation to each other and in the context of time as received.

The last 60 or so years of automation have been closely associated with the practice and technology of computing. Automation goes beyond "automatic" in the sense of adding feedback and sensing to a process. A clock is automatic. A computer-aided manufacturing line can be a form of automation. However, computing is that aspect of automation that deals with digital data. Automation has suffered the same way that information has suffered: too many uses, and they do not all conspire to inspire.

COMPUTING IS SOFTWARE

The first computers did not have software as we know it. They were hardwired. Software made what might be a called a giant calculator into a computer we might recognize—a general purpose "think" machine. Software made it possible to have application programs that could complete tasks such as accounting, order entry, and word processing.

Use of software is an assumed process. If you asked a fish how it liked the water, it would, if it could talk, find your question meaningless, as water is all it knows. The same in some ways can be said for our life in software. We use it and it sustains us, or at least we think so and act so. However, there were once computers without software. There were computers without internal programming. Internal programming had to be invented, mostly by the mathematician John von Neumann. Software had to be invented. Software became the applied internal program that, once invented, could be reapplied. It is essentially a series of automated algorithms that control and prescribe individual actions such as word processing, spreadsheets, and computer graphics.

A WAY OF LIFE

Software has become our way of life, and is ever more so with an aggressive enterprise. It is a means of controlling, communicating, and storing information. It is, if used intelligently, an opportunity to maintain a command position or at least to remain competitive. Software, like any automation, expedites but does not of itself solve anything. Persons or companies or nations that want solutions have to start by determining what they want using their brains. The computing activity can assist the brain process, but not replace it.

A VERY SHORT HISTORY

Software grew up over a period of 50 years. It is still growing up. The computers expedite the software while the software expedites the processes and the businesses. We might ask what does going digital do to information. It takes information in packets (bits and bytes)—reducing information to automatable units. This works in computers, cameras, cell phones, and now billions of objects. Digital information is increasing in amount, as we have observed, and dominates information communication as we experience it today.

The increase translates into a growing problem. In order to respond intelligently to increased consumer demand, more information is being processed. Information is being processed from global sources, from huge inputs from RFID tagging and recording, from tracking analysis, and from countless other origins. It is creating data or information torrents. These torrents are not singular; there are many rivers of information that flow into any company. Information is pulsing through the synthetic veins, channels, wires, and wireless communication devices relentlessly. The flow may become a flood, however, if there are inadequate storage facilities. A data warehouse is a library of databases that acts as a depository and reference tool for massive amounts of data. The supply chain as it operates on a global scale requires massive amounts of data processing to track, to move through customs, to regulate price, and to meet the demands of the Sarbanes-Oxley rules of business transactions.

INFORMING

The greatest change in managing information over the past three decades is the degree to which the informing is done by computer. Now the informing is done through Internet services. These advances have modified, even revolutionized, the processes and business of transporting, retailing, and manufacturing. Competitive business is now done through the melding of many complex software uses that serve as functioning modules for everything from quality control to use of labor, routing, machine setup, and materials and product flow through the factory, warehouse, or distribution center. The computer has pressed the decision-making activity of business into a real-time activity, or something as close to real time as possible. The boss can now maintain an awareness of the details of each and every process, as can the other officers and plant manager.

All of these players can all be at the decision table at the same time with their own particular versions of the critical information of business. The president gets a big picture, and can drill down for a more detailed perspective if he or she desires. The financial officer can get elaborate metrics, and yet is also able to get lower level specifics of nonfinancial data. Information is packaged into understandable and user-directed formats.

BABYING A PRODUCT

The same information-informing changes occur, and have intense effects, within the flow of manufacturing as in manufacturing a new product—from planning to design, modification, testing, and ease of manufacture; as with manufacture to marketing, distribution, sales, customer service, return, and iterations. As in emergency oil rig capping, management must act in real time—synchronized, collaborative, and a part of an ongoing process of modifying (training, redesign, and other necessary changes).

The recent creation of product lifecycle management (PLM), or the means to see products and their development from origin through modification and to termination, has given a context within which management can operate more intelligently. It offers the long view and at the same time offers the means to plan, organize, execute, and track products through origination to maturity. Product lifecycle management development is, by its very nature, a team activity, involving planners, designers, marketers, manufacturers, and salespeople. Those who accept a synchronous and adaptive course of action select a team, assign roles to the team or accept pre-existing roles, accept the sharing of control, learn through training to synchronize, and learn to adapt to situations as they come up in real time. These can involve reacting to competitive products, manufacturing constraints, market trends, or internal financial realities. PLM is another way into the supply chain, because each product (and its sourcing, transport, manufacture, and distribution) is a key to successfully marketing a product over its life cycle.

STORAGE AND TRANSIT GROW UP

Software products directed at particular functions have multiplied like rabbits, and they are increasingly necessary as the complexities of trade multiply. Early users of such products have both an advantage and disadvantage. The early adoption of a new system can be costly, as the software may have glitches; yet by being an early practitioner of intelligent software, the company may gain market advantage.

The managing of goods in a warehouse is now a complex act that involves the warehouse personnel, the suppliers to the warehouse, the receiver (eventually of goods), and other interested parties such as accounting, tax officials, compliance organizations, etc. Warehouse management systems (WMS) software has grown up with the changes in inventory control and tracking. A WMS offers a company the opportunity to know what is in the warehouse, when it arrived, when it is expected to leave, its nature (material, part, product, manufacturer, etc.), and its cost. It allows the company to direct actions involving these stored materials as electronic requests (orders) come in and have to be fulfilled.

The process of governing the transit of goods is a lot more than trucks, railroads, and sea-lanes. It is compliance, taxation, customs, security, insurance, language, timing, spacing, and a host of other factors. This has meant the evolution of transportation management software (TMS) and logistics management software. These may be an extension of a large-scale set of enterprise resource planning (ERP) software applications, or a system of its own that is useful for third-party logistics providers that want to computerize their business (or, more likely, recomputerize it). ERP is the backbone of a manufacturing enterprise. The pressure of ERP has brought many other software applications into being. ERP is directly or indirectly responsible for the emergence of warehouse managing systems, product lifecycle management, transportation management systems, and service-oriented architecture (SOA). The latter is a network-based set of interoperable software applications that provide insight and control over a large array of services. ERP, as the backbone software of a company, acts in concert with all of these applications.

MORE BANG FOR YOUR BUCK

Applications from big ERP providers such as SAP and IFS often spread out into many territories of application. It is a dashboard-style program (a computer software application that gives constantly updated metric in graphic form) that informs a manager of the metrics of sales.

Business activity management (BAM) is coming to logistics and the supply chain as well. BAM is a software application that helps monitor business activity and processing using information received on a computer screen to analyze key events or results that are summarized, and also to provide alerts concerning alarm situations, such as a drop off in sales or a delay in delivery. There is clearly a growing executive requirement for speed in timely management as to where materials are and where they're going. This has spurred the growth of a whole new set of applications. It is the latest electronic method of keeping close tabs on your business and everything that goes into running it. BAM was developed to provide senior executives a dashboard review on a single computer screen of what a company looks like in its processes.

As an example, one provider of BAM for logistics, Wakefield, Massachusetts–based Edgewater Technology, has worked with the Logistics Group, a major third-party logistics provider, with complex transportation systems. They reduced the number of lost packages by 75 percent with their package-tracking component. At the same time, Edgewater cut $8.5 million from its clients' operating costs within the first year. The Logistics Group also has experienced a substantial increase in efficiency and customer satisfaction.

Activity-monitoring techniques are able to manage even small-scale, day-to-day operations more efficiently and economically. A key, according to the providers, is to increase the speed, accuracy, and access to information that is presented to decision makers. BAM software technology can provide logistics executives with maps, charts, and graphs that are used to show activity from an overall perspective or for specific interests. BAM technologies in logistics and supply-chain management may be helping companies become more competitive in meeting global needs of just-in-time manufacturing and sales. One reason for the adoption of BAM today is regulatory compliance that requires business transactions to be monitored more closely. In addition, RFID and telemetry for logistics require monitoring of large volumes of data that cannot be handled by traditional reporting and analysis tools. Manufacturers are starting to use BAM to track supply chain activities in real time.

SERVICE-ORIENTED APPLICATIONS

As the need for loosely coupled software services has become apparent, the software industry has responded with software that answers an enterprise's needs for networked, on-demand solutions. This software is not directly tied to any specific technology. The whole point is to make a range of other software interoperable. The world of on-demand service through the Internet has brought about a whole new breed of software such as SOA. These software applications tie together services such as ordering of goods, fulfillment, credit checks, and financial transactions.

Another ship in the armada of supply chain and logistics software is global trade managing (GTM). This robust software is able to manage the major factors governing global trade with suppliers (manufacturers, processors); partners, such as carriers and third-party logistics providers; wholesalers; and retailers. The new scale, and the new complexity of world trade, makes such a managing system a necessity.

BEYOND SOFTWARE

Despite the advantage of distributed control and shared information, manufacturing managers cannot always control the seasons. They can't always increase productivity. They can't always determine the nature and the moves of the competition. They can't always make a measurable gain in quality. They can't always cut costs—and may have to increase them. They can't always procure the right things at the right time in the right place. There are limits to even the best, most robust, and more comprehensive software system.

SUMMING UP: AUTOMATING AND COMPUTING

Automating and computing appear to be joined at the hip, enablers of each other. One can't be without the other. The range of automation and the range of computing services and networks now available to the supply chain manager or the logistics VP are formidable. Internet-enabled networks now have global reach and global consequence. Running any business within the supply chain world today is computer dependent, automation oriented, and has the Internet as an essential support.

Chapter 7

THE WORLD IS ALWAYS WITH US: COMMUNICATION

COMMUNICATING BEFORE COMMUNICATING

Nobody "communicated" in the old days. As far as I know, the word wasn't used until the 14th century in Europe. It was probably not a part of the vernacular of a typical person until the mid-20th century. We can't imagine Shakespeare writing, "Hamlet, shall thou communicate with Laertes?" Communication is now beyond the use of our ordinary senses. It has been analyzed and codified and has benefited from the development of technology that makes remote communication possible both visually and verbally. What most people were not prepared for was the conversion of the computer from a mere automatic typewriter to a tool that allows us a full range of communication on a global basis.

IT TOOK SHANNON

The late Claude Shannon saw and acted where others neither saw nor acted. He articulated the division between sender, communicator (or media), and receiver in a paper entitled "A Mathematical Theory of Communication," and communication was never the same again. He introduced to the world a rather simple abstraction that consisted of describing the process of communication as a channel. This channel was made up of three elements: the information source or sender (such as a telegraph operator), a medium of transmission (the telegraph wire with its distortion and noise), and the receiver (another telegraph person) that reconstructs the message—in this case, Morse code.

Shannon's construct is the basis of telephone messages and now messages over the Internet. A majority of supply chain and logistics messages have his basic construct operating through new technology such as wireless messages and secure networks on the Internet.

IT TOOK INVENTORS TO HELP US COMMUNICATE

It took many inventors and inventions to make the world of modern communication feasible, such as Samuel Morse's code, Thomas Edison's photograph, Charles Steinmetz's understanding of alternating current, and Alexander Graham Bell's telephone. After carrier pigeon, semaphore, smoke signals, packet boats, horse-delivered mail, and human messengers, it took a wire and a magnet-driven telegraph to change messaging forever. The invention of the telegraph led to the laying of transatlantic cable and the establishment of Western Union offices in all major cities. It led to stringing wire across America and most of Europe. It required a code and those able to send and receive the code. This made it not sufficiently pervasive for the average citizen, as they could not have it in their homes or master its form. But it did expedite rail schedules and deliveries. The first steps in supply control were established.

Alexander Graham Bell made the wire talk by using a magnetic diaphragm that mimicked sound spoken against it. The telephone was not just a means of sending a voice or a sound over a wire; it was a means to give ordinary people access to each other using their voices and their ears. It made the telegraph a specialist system.

Guglielmo Marconi's 1901 invention of a radio that could transmit Morse code across the ocean leapfrogged the telegraph and the telephone to an extent. The march of messaging and connecting technology had been relentless between Morse's time and Marconi's. Ever since Morse, it has been fair game to improve communications. This means, in order of priority, messaging faster and more cheaply.

COMPUTERS AND COMMUNICATING

The merger of computing and the telephone, wireless communication, and the facsimile machine led to a period in supply and logistics that uses what is called electronic data interchange (EDI). EDI has two meanings: It is the standard by which electronically communicated business information is formatted. It can structure functions such as purchasing orders. It is also the descriptor for the process of communicating electronically. Although pre-Internet, it is still used as a means by which one business electronically connects to another to place an order, list bills of materials, or exchange other information such as quotes.

A turning point in computing came in 1969, when a young MIT student, Leonard Kleinrock, applied queuing theory to data packaging for computer-to-computer communication. Kleinrock thought up the idea of demand access, the beginning of what would become on-demand supply chains. He felt you only should have demand when you needed it. This meant that no one switch controlled the traffic of the system, but all shared equally in their traffic. The data in packets would line up in the queue as they arrived, hang around, and leave. This meant there would be distributed control in computer-to-computer networks, unlike the technique of circuit switching as used in telephone systems. Telephones use dedicated lines, and do not allow for another party or queuing except for special operations such as conference calling.

COMMUNICATION REVOLUTION

This structure of computer-to-computer communication is, by way of being, a revolution. The very nature of the Internet, by user-managed messages in packets that offer distributed control, is the basis for on-demand supply chain technology and practice. One person, or customer, can on demand use the network to request from a supplier—or a company with sources of supply—what they want, see it delivered, and watch it in its delivery cycle. Intelligent companies build their business upon intelligent response through this means.

Many other people gave direction to the development of what in time became the Internet. The government system evolved into a university-based communication system and that, in time, grew to what we know today. Dr. Paul Baran was responsible for separating the data into small bits like a postcard or a Morse signal. Tim Berners-Lee was the creator of the World Wide Web (WWW), and Ray Tomlinson was the inventor of email. They should go on the list of those who deserve greater recognition.

ARTHUR CLARKE AND SATELLITE COMMUNICATIONS

The idea of bouncing communication off of a strategically placed Earth satellite was first posed in 1945 by one of our finest science fiction writers, Arthur C. Clarke, who also wrote *2001: A Space Odyssey*. There is nothing fictional about satellite communication. It is, along with cell towers, a key to wireless communication. Will there be, in time, any other kind of communication? Isn't Clarke's idea how logistics tracking works? Isn't Clarke's idea how this on-demand software really comes to be useful?

This Internet in turn has become the heart of business communication that allows for one customer to ask the world for the best price, the best product, and the best delivery.

In this demanding world, the old empires of place give way to new networks of space. The old-style hierarchical management of a General Motors gives way to the surging creativity of Google, Dell Computer, Wal-Mart, Yahoo!, Apple Computer, and eBay. They avoid too many levels of management and the bureaucracy this entails. They share, in most cases, information from top to bottom, with the same information access for the CEO as for the supervisor of a plant or a store. They operate closely tied to the demands of the customer, and not of the boss. These companies are carving out a new Web-based economics, a new way of communicating in business, and a new means of working, living, and marketing.

A TWIN BIRTH

The supply chain and the Internet grew up together. The ability to connect to parties all over the Earth had to wait for the Internet to provide a vehicle for parties all over the Earth to share written communication, image communication, spreadsheet data, and even videos or movies. The utility of the Internet was accelerated by the development of today's supply chain. Joined at birth, they encourage each other: The Internet enables the supply chain to take on new proportions, and the supply chain makes the Internet a more vital tool in global business.

On-demand software, eBay, Google, Amazon.com, and a thousand software applications couldn't make it over TV, the telephone, or even on the computer, until it added communication capability. It took the Internet. People and companies could now research, communicate, make deals, organize contracts, track products, and acknowledge orders and receipt.

THE GLOBAL SILK ROAD

The Internet does not have physical substance as perceived by the user. But the Internet requires hundreds of thousands of servers to accommodate the transactions. Google is said to have over 450,000 servers. There is a cost, but the cost is, to a great extent, transparent to the average user. Internet communication can be recorded, audited, played back, edited, transformed, and shared. It opens doors. The combination of provider, medium, and controller with receiver expedites business and communication worldwide. More to the point, it opens minds, and I think that is what those who developed the Web over the last 50 years had as their objective.

RFID BY SATELLITE

Another level of communication today is RFID technology, which can be used throughout the supply chain. It is a not a substitute for bar codes so much as it is an extension of what bar codes can do. By satellite, RFID systems can connect to manufacturing facilities and source tag the goods, parts, or products and the pallets, packages, or containers that contain them. By satellite, RFID can connect to overseas shipments as tags inside containers, and through this, determine the condition, temperature, and security level of the load. By satellite, RFID can connect to the port and act to enable customs data to be processed, or control inventory of loads. By satellite, RFID can connect to the carriers or third-party freight forwarders—those intermediaries in the transportation process. This is really information access, process, and delivery control.

RFID can also connect to ground transportation at a destination, giving the shipment status, the location in motion or at destination, the estimated time of delivery, the vehicle's content, and the routing of driver and his or her scheduling. RFID can connect to a warehouse or distribution center to gather or send data about docking, gates, yards, and their management. RFID can connect to an RFID retailer for inventory control or antitheft status. RFID can connect to the customer via phone, computer link, or wireless device such as a PDA to communicate the status of a requested order.

Modern manufacturers, retailers, and carriers are very much in tune with the generative aspect of these RFID process winners. That means being networked, operating in real time, and communicating and responding digitally. RFID has inspired many breaking technologies that are bound to have a complex impact on communications as we now know it. Virtual operational data store (VODS) should make the processing of information faster and less cumbersome by enabling users to own fewer volumes. Value added networks (VANs) will enhance information processing through leasing of service and are more like the networks of energy sharing today. There will also be advances in EPCGlobal (electronic product code), and as it becomes more universally accepted, it will have a slingshot effect in speeding up tracking and identification.

BUSINESS ADVANTAGE

Businesses (and specifically the carriers) that process in real time, just-in-time, and in synchronous action are the winners in the marketplace. The technologies that have multiplied from the computer and its networking have made it possible to deliver these advantages. New technologies become more and more dominant, faster and faster, and ubiquitous.

Today's business isn't just about things and places. Having many vehicles is a requirement for a major commerce player, but it's not an advantage until they are dealt with as a fleet. A fleet, like an armada, is as good as its control and coordination. The British invented this concept in the days of sailing ships. They combined a keen sense of time with the availability and use of fast packet boats for distant messages and semaphore for close communication. Today, wireless communication connects trucks to hubs to rail to air. UPS, FedEx, DHL, and third-party logistics providers' trucks are communication stations in motion, as is shipping by sea and air. As it has evolved, the communications of the truck and its driver/manager has nearly overwhelmed in importance their driving functions.

WEB-BASED SOLUTIONS

In less than 50 years, we have, gone from many streets draped with multiple wires and endless ungainly telephone poles to a telephone technology that uses orbiting satellites and no poles. A business has to embrace these changes to stay *au courant*. There are no monopolies on the control of and understanding of change. The ability to change is as fluid and restless as mercury. The ability to change a business is only viable while operating the business in real time with partners.

Yes, as they said in many a corny movie: synchronize your watches. The new adaptive enterprise has to be organized around synchronized activity with active distributed control to capitalize on change, and not just simply modify incrementally existing business procedures. Being adaptive means having "sensing" near and far. It means responding to the detection of environmental change, business competition change, market change, and internal change (e.g., too much inventory, too slow a delivery, too high a price). It means responding with a more than adequate change in the metrics of orders, sales, and manufacture. It means being prepared for whatever change in strategy, tactic, or practice is required to solve the problem at hand.

NO COMPANY IS AN ISLAND

No company is big enough to go it alone. Even Wal-Mart has partners, and the basis of the partnership is communication—communication along a secure Internet connection. It partners with companies such as Procter & Gamble on developing RFID technology. It partners with 3PLs on logistics. It partners by collaborating within its supply chain with truckers and shippers.

IBM operates in a similar manner, and collaborates with Maersk Line on shipping and with a host of middleware suppliers that organize information-processing aspects of logistics and the supply chain in a global context.

Commerce companies also partner extensively. UPS, for instance, has bought Mail Boxes Etc. (now known as the UPS Store), while FedEx bought Kinko's in 2004.

GOING WIRELESS

Disengaging ourselves from wired connections and endless plugs (in all their configurations and power cables or transformers, none of which are transferable) should be a blessing. Wireless communication will now connect between objects with objects, objects with people, people with objects, and people with people. The car gave us ground mobility. The truck gave us ground goods mobility. The Internet gives us real mobility. We find ourselves connecting by disconnecting. It is the wireless revolution in communication.

The power of the Web is a constant surprise and often a good one. Surely we are just beginning to find out how we might take advantage of this global network of information and opportunity.

An example is the emergence of eManufacturing, a major defining element in this march toward an electronic future and more and more the central subject of business generally. However, there are projects of a smaller nature but nonetheless exciting. Let us examine one way that is now available and look at a few others that may, in time, have functional and economic merit.

EMANUFACTURING

It is possible today to design a part and have it manufactured, all using the Internet. An actual offering, eMachineShop.com, does just this. The site allows a user to download a computer-aided drafting (CAD) program backed by artificial intelligence (AI) power. The AI assist helps the user expedite his or her design and acts as an intelligent advisor on what can and cannot be done as to a radius or a fillet, for instance, in a particular design for a particular method of manufacture; it's like having an analysis performed by a machining expert. In other words, it makes the design capable of best practice machining or manufacturing.

The system allows for the design and manufacture of parts such as enclosures, electronic panels, parts for optical devices, and scientific instruments. This technology allows users at all skill levels and fields to create custom parts without consulting an expert.

What is most fascinating is that eMachineShop can handle anything from an order of one to an order of up to a million. The cost of the job can be calculated automatically during the design process, and a user can see how a change in design or materials will affect the final cost. This allows the user to get the best design and the best price combination. It allows even the smallest companies to simplify, customize, and expedite their supply chains.

PRODUCTS ON DEMAND

We have already gotten used to the idea of ordering a customized computer from a supplier such as Dell. We have also found that we can order an automobile customized to our taste from an auto dealer. These orders fit right into the make-to-order philosophy and strategy becoming so popular today among manufacturers and their application support vendors.

One future example of such a service would be eWorkcells. This still imaginary service would go a step further and build a robot work cell from parts that fulfill the customer's specifications. This would allow for structural parts that build from specific user needs the cell and its robot, the controller, end-effectors, and materials-handling equipment or special equipment (as for welding or packaging). Because work cells most often come in multiples, this would allow for repeat business or variations on the original specification.

An existing company, eManufacturing, Inc., specializes in electronic, control, and instrumentation virtual manufacturing. It offers several different levels of service such as design and build, turnkey, and assemble-only. It manufactures in India by electronic communication and thereby becomes a unique type of outsourcing.

All of these actualities and possibilities are a form of outsourcing, but outsourcing with a difference.

SUMMING UP: COMMUNICATING

The simple means of early communication gave way to communication as a science through the work of Shannon. In a headlong rush, communication technology has created a shell of networked messaging that girdles our Earth. This electronic shell from cell tower and satellite offers smart companies and individuals the opportunity to research, plan, source, transport, manufacture, deliver, market, and sell products, parts, materials, and services. In many ways, it levels the playing field: Small entrepreneurs anywhere can use the services of large global operations to extend their reach and line their pockets. If you want to succeed in this environment, you must learn to think in new terms, visualize concepts on new scales, and work within new communication realities.

Part Two

SUPPLY CHAIN EVOLUTION

The supply chain has its antecedents and systems that contributed to its potential: on the sea with fleets of ships, ports, trade lanes; on the rails with right of way, stations, yards, and, in time, intermodal capability; in the air with aircraft, airports, and hubs; and on the ground with trucks, road systems, and warehousing and distribution centers. Wars have had the effect of accelerating the creation of logistics and the need for coordinated business and physical processes globally. Key concepts such as the shipping container, the fork lift, and the bar code have made it possible to move more goods in less time to more places. The advent of the computer and communication technology has ratcheted up all of these modes and devices to an ever more vast supply chain world today. Companies such as Wal-Mart, IKEA, Dell, and Intel have used their insights into supply chain strategies to advance their businesses aggressively.

Chapter 8

THE HISTORY OF THE SUPPLY CHAIN

Until the Middle Ages, things primarily moved by ox and donkey. Horses moved people and some carts, but weren't used for long trips or heavy materials. The supplies being moved were bundled, rope-lashed, or wrapped in cloth or leather. There were barrels, jars for liquids, baskets of all sizes and shapes, and nets for gathering odd things. Cardboard crates as we know them today did not exist until the early 20th century.

The products being moved were the creation of craftspeople and artisans, or farmers and miners. There was none of the industry that we take for granted today, but there was vast trade in time between China and Rome, and between Rome and its colonies. Need almost always exceeded supply; the idea of an on-demand system had no references and no application. Feast and famine were familiar rounds from Roman times through the Middle Ages. The early seeds of outsourcing were not so much consequences of a business decision as they were the result of simply not having the necessary supplies locally. Rome had to be fed grain from abroad; its need for tin and wood required a great deal of scrounging. Britain served for metals and Gaul, Germania, and Hispania served for grain.

INFRASTRUCTURES CAN WORK BOTH WAYS

The Romans built a great road system to supply their troops in an ever-expanding Empire. Those same roads were used by their enemies to attack and sack Rome. The British Empire's success depended on its navy, and the navy depended on a clock's ability to tell its navigators where a ship was geographically. John Harrison's famous set of clocks gave them the setting of longitude—and, consequently, Australia, India, New Zealand, Canada, Bermuda, and almost the American colonies.

Technology and disease change war and supply more than troops do. This means that a technology can transform an infrastructure and the supply chain dependent upon it. An infrastructure and the supply chain can stimulate new forms of technology.

SLAVES AS MACHINES OF THE DAY

The early cultures did not outsource manufacturing, as there was no manufacturing by our standards. Craftsmen and local slaves made things. Today, cheap labor is a huge driving force for outsourcing. Then, the cheap labor was slaves and artisans who were on the lowest level of society. The Roman Empire had millions of slaves. To some degree, the huge presence of slaves discouraged Rome from any large-scale incursion into technology applied to manufacturing or commerce. In the long run, slavery was self-defeating.

The Romans applied technical understanding to building in concrete, to road structure, to sewers and water systems, and to military weapons. There were the equivalent of captains of trade, modest middlemen, and lots of slaves to do the lifting.

MECHANICAL ADVANTAGE

Mechanical advantage with levers, pulleys, and inclined planes became known only slowly. By Roman times, water was used to grind flour, and by the Middle Ages, water was used to run foundries, presses, and other heavy-duty metal work. Retailing was at best primitive. Traders set up shop in open markets and bazaars. The growth of cities offered shops along streets and associated with forums in Rome and the large cities of the Middle East.

Bean counters in Mesopotamian times (5000 B.C.) had there own equivalent of the "bar code" in the form of clay pictograms that were most often used to keep records. The Romans used wax tablets in the same way. There was no means of scanning the handwritten lists, other than with the eyes. If you wanted to know where your jars of honey or fish sauce happened to be at the moment, you would be out of luck.

ALL ROADS LED TO ROME

A horsed messenger in Roman times could take a week to collect and deliver a message. With their system of roads, Romans did manage under pressure to deliver a message as far as 150 miles in one day (as fast as the short-lived U.S. Pony Express). The Romans did this by assigning priority to a messenger. The messenger from an emperor or senator would be given priority that allowed through passage and placed others either off the road or to the side. It is like having an express lane on a highway today.

The idea of the road as we know it came directly from the Romans. There were early roads in China, India, and Central America, but Roman roads were the first to have underlayment, culverts, bridges, horse posting houses, and mile markers. Roman roads started several centuries before Christ. The Roman highways lasted as the essential roads of Europe into the 17th century. Their highways were a part of a much more complex infrastructure that supported the use of the highway. This consisted of economic taxation for repair, maintenance, and control of bridges, culverts, and drains.

EUROPE GETS STEAMED UP

In the Middle Ages, the peasant and serf became the substitute for the slave. The development of transportation, messaging, and manufacture didn't essentially change between A.D. 400 and 1500. In time, however, the Renaissance brought together forces that led to the inauguration of science and its practical side, technology.

The 1712 steam engine changed the existing world just as the Internet is changing ours. The industrial revolution, spearheaded by the steam engine, saw the advent of wooden rails in deep mines made possible by the raising of water by steam power. The wooden rails soon became metal. The revolution saw the tooling of wood and metal by steam-powered machines and, in time, steam ships and rail took off.

French soldiers used the word *loger* to mean to *lodge*. In or around the year 1861, the process of moving supplies in and out of the barracks became known as *logistiques*. During the period of 1790 to 1946, France was consistently in a war, between wars, or recovering from a war. It needed massive supply lines to arm and feed its troops.

LINCOLN GOT IT RIGHT

The American Civil War was the testing ground for a new style of war, conducted with the full support of the railroad, of highly developed industrial factories, and of such novelties as Morse's successful 1844 telegraph. The Civil War was the first to use ironclad ships, balloons for observation, and submarines. Goods and messages were moved in volume over thousands of miles by rails, local roads, canals, rivers, and ocean. Steamships (or ships with steam and sail) dominated sea traffic by the end of the war. Arsenals and goods depots were more and more the precursors of modern warehouses and distribution centers. The Civil War was the first war that applied technology, as we know it, to the process of war.

LOGISTICS GOES TO THE CIRCUS

In the late 19th century, the Ringling Brothers and Barnum & Bailey Circus became a city unto itself: a portable tent city. A traveling circus like this one traveled, set up, entertained, and broke camp, as if by magic. It was an early example of timed logistics in planning delivery and action.

The technology used in the circus was basically borrowed from sailing ships and consisted of rigging, masts, and stays that supported the structures of the circus tents. Wagons and railcars supplemented these. The circus managers became experts at the process of erecting and dismantling the circus, and even put the elephants to work. It was coordinated work that looked complex, but was simplified by craft and a learned system. Each crew had a boss, and each crew member was responsible for a series of the tasks. All of the crews worked simultaneously. There was a sequence to everything; each job had its art, its timing, and its sequence.

Workers loaded and unloaded the circus rail cars by a ramp that allowed animals to enter or leave a boxcar. The ramp became a universal method of loading that was, and still is, referred to as "circus ramping" by railroaders.

FROM THE CIRCUS TO THE BATTLEFIELD

The German Officer Corps applied the emerging science of logistics to its movement of goods and troops and subsequent supply in World War I, and later in support of its World War II blitzkrieg. Trucks using diesel engines invented by Rudolf Diesel came to be in 1892 and were the forerunners of the engines in big rigs; they soon became the means of goods transfer from rail to truck and ship to truck in peace and war. In 1907, Jim Casey started UPS in Seattle; in 1908, Henry Ford introduced the Model T and in 1913, the Ford Motor Company began using mass production to build its automobiles and, soon, its pickup trucks.

It is in the nature of war that all supplies are in short supply. Rationing and military emergencies dominated the World War I supply chain. World War I allies and the Germans substituted trucks and trains for horses as much as possible. U.S. ships were jury-rigged to accommodate troops or supplies. There was no time to design and build shipping or trucking for transport. Specially designed war vehicles and ships were restricted to naval ships and army tanks.

OVER THERE, SEND THE WORD: *LOGISTICS*

Volume and speed were the watchwords. The U.S. expeditionary force in World War I was two million strong and had to be armed, fed, and clothed daily. It was the largest logistics operation in the world up to that time. The word *logistics* had not traveled well. The U.S. Army and Navy used various forms of the words *supply* and *procurement* to refer to inventory, movement, and handling.

Soon after World War I, the forklift truck was invented. Crude lifts dated to the late 19th century, as did the first motorized cranes. Without cranes and forklifts, almost nothing would move in our mechanical world of today.

By World War II, the word *logistics* was in place. World War II was to a great extent won by the Allies through superior logistics and massive U.S. manufacturing, with massive numbers of war instruments delivered to the front in record time, and with plenty of fuel. This feat was a precursor of overnight delivery by UPS, FedEx, and DHL and the handling of massive numbers of different goods, as with Wal-Mart. The war had an additional contribution: Goods needed to be specific to special orders. Supplies to the South Pacific were geared to that climate and that war. Supplies to Europe had other factors that made supply seasonal and customer-centric. Global logistics was born out of war.

AMERICAN INGENUITY

The United States carried on a two-ocean war on several continents, and supplied its Army, Navy, and Marine Corps better than any other army. It also supplied Britain, Russia, and other smaller-scale allies such as the Free French from its home base, primarily by ship. The Liberty ship, the most heavily produced cargo ship of the period, became an icon in its time. Its manufacture was an activity that set up many assembly docks, supplied them with many parts, and used labor only where necessary. The builders of the Liberty ship innovated: They poured the hulls in concrete forms, dropped the pre-made steel ship superstructure into the concrete hulls, and soon thereafter sailed off.

Mass production meant that the ships were too plentiful to sink; the supplies got through, and in this manner, volumes of low-tech freighters defeated high-tech U-boats. The high-tech U-boats were subsequently defeated by high-tech sonar and radar widely distributed in scans by aircraft and destroyers.

It is important to know when a technology should be high or low. In a crude way, concrete and cheaply made ships in great supply defeated forces who were working with more advanced technologies. It was not a question of how many ships could be sunk, but it was a question of how many ships were not sunk. This rule of negation might well be applied to many supply chain situations as an effective means to gain strategic advantage in business. In any contest, the thing to watch is not how many of the opponent (e.g., other team, company, etc.) are done in, but what percentage of gain they have against you.

The World War II period also saw the first great national road system since ancient Rome, the autobahn. It defined the nature of a modern highway and must have been well observed by occupying

American forces. It used many of the techniques of later highways, including no grade crossing by railroads or other roads, and bridges over the highway to afford neighborhood linkages.

A period of great advances followed the end of World War II; many of these would create the tools and systems that would one day be our modern logistics and its supply chain. In 1946, George Devol created the industrial robot. The Toyota Production System built up steam from the day the war was over, while in 1949 the micro revolution started with the invention of the transistor. In 1952, a patent for the bar code was granted; it was first used to identify railroad cars.

IKE'S PIKES

General Dwight D. Eisenhower saw the autobahn and its advantages while defeating Germany. The United States' system of roadways was built after the successful Federal-Aid Highway Act of 1956, and became the system of interstate highways we know today. It matched the length of the Roman road system (approximately 50,000 miles), but took a relatively short three decades to complete.

It took a highway to create national road shipping in any real sense. Rail service did span the nation, but at the end of the track, there had to be an intermodal operation that transferred the goods from one transportation mode to another. The existence of Eisenhower's highways made trucking a national activity. The United States was suddenly laced together by roads that could handle heavy goods using 18-wheelers—and in some ways, just in time, as the birth of supermarkets and malls was underway. Push manufacturing found its delivery solution and its retailing solution at least temporarily. Push manufacturing was manufacturing at the behest of the manufacturer in an era when people clamored for new cars, refrigerators, and TVs. High production was the goal, whereas with time, a shift occurred. Rather than the manufacturer making decisions about what would be available, the customer demanded specific types of products, and this became what is now called pull manufacturing and economics.

A NEW KIND OF HIGHWAY

The infrastructure of bridges, exit ramps, highway service stations, and other support structures came into place. Mom-and-pop trucking companies were spawned across the entire nation. They worked side by side with other logistics businesses that had fleets of trucks or rail companies that owned not only the rail cars but also the track system and the beginnings of intermodal transportation on a grand scale. Commercial air companies such as Pan Am and TWA also began carrying freight in the lower holds of their passenger planes. It was the beginning of airfreight forwarding. Airfreight forwarding is a service that may use owned aircraft, as is the case of FedEx, UPS, and a few commercial airlines, or it may, as with a third-party logistics provider, lease space from a commercial air carrier. The freight forwarder picks up and prepares the air load, taking responsibility for tracking, customs, and whatever complications might arise; this process can include using distribution centers and warehousing facilities.

Today there are four million miles of roads and highways in the United States. Of these, about 1 percent are of the level of an interstate highway. The rest range from dirt roads to multilane highways without the interstate amenities (no grade crossings, ramp exits, median dividers, etc.). Only Germany has a higher level of road construction than the United States, but in many ways, the U.S. system is grossly inadequate and is not evolving quickly enough to meet the needs of modern logistics.

MALCOLM MCLEAN'S CONTAINERS

In World War II transport, ships, trucks, jeeps, and many other delivery means were designed specifically for the job at hand. At-home logistics in World War II meant more economical consumer transport, reduced delivery of nonessentials, and a consumer economy on hold. During the course of the next war in Korea, the United States developed a system of very large boxes (almost the size of a railroad car) that became the forerunners of the shipping containers we know today; modern containers were developed by Malcolm McLean in 1956, creating the need for containerships. These containers became the means of supply first for the war in Vietnam. They have since become the worldwide means for product trading delivery and 200,000,000 containers travel around the Earth yearly.

TILT!

The use of highways and trucks, planes and airports, ships and containers is not enough to explain the surge in trade and the efficiency of that trade. The year 1956 also saw the first flat package design from IKEA in Sweden. The world had arrived at a new level of business. As the shift occurred from a push economy to a pull economy, the processing and communication of information became a major factor in manufacturing, commerce, and retailing.

As competition increased between companies and as global trade expanded, quality control became an important issue. Faster product development became a concern. Better coordination between design and manufacturing, between orders and fulfillment, and between delivery time promised and delivery time executed became significant business concerns. Is it any wonder that in 1969, DHL was founded, and two years later, FedEx?

SUPPLY CHAIN TOOK OVER J-I-T MANTLE

The supply chain, as distinct from logistics, is the sequence of business decisions (e.g., orders, inventory, payment plan, level of priority) and business functions (e.g., supply, transport, warehouse, manufacture), and their interrelations. The individual parts have been with us for millennia, but they were not named, defined, and made into a system, as we now know it, until the latter part of the 20th century. The supply chain combined with modern-day logistics is the supercharged engine of response to the changing opportunities and challenges of today's business. The supply chain and logistics as concepts are growing and changing daily, and UPS, FedEx, DHL, and other 3PLs are major change agents. The supply chain (with a core of new logistics practices) is the defining concept behind the final evolution of a push economy to a pull economy. The conception of the process has shifted to have the consumer as its center, and the supply chain became the connection.

Warehouse management and execution systems were developed alongside manufacturing basics such as MRP, and later ERP, that not only ran the processes of manufacturing but also extended out to supplier management and distribution management. So, we have not just logistics now but supply chains.

SUMMING UP: LOGISTICS

We now have the supply chain as an extension of logistics practice and logistics as an outgrowth of the push style of manufacturing. To a great extent, logistics is the stepchild of war, as war makes the transport of goods as vital as the transport of troops. The supply chain, before the word was coined, was referred to as the supply line or procurement, and was the lifeblood of any military effort. Business today in all its ramifications uses the devices and strategies of Barnum, World War I, World War II, the Korean War, and Desert Storm. The supply chain has become an integrating concept that ties together the individual logistical events. It is the glue to which business profit sticks.

Chapter

9

LIFT THAT BALE: TRANSPORT BY GROUND, AIR, SEA, AND RAIL

Where are we are now in logistics? The advent of pull in commerce did not happen automatically or in a neat and short time frame. Pull has been assembled from many parts in an organic way, and not as a bright idea giving immediate insight and opportunity. Pull in commerce came only after a long preamble and an intense period of its opposite, push. People for centuries moved goods, tools, and supplies without a thought as to what they were doing in any abstract way. It took the arduous development of logistics and the recognition that a supply chain might be a good thing.

We are now in a logistic wonder world that deals with everything from frozen partridges to multiton steam generators; a living killer whale; 700,000 bottles of wine by UPS; 2,500,000 cans of Heineken safely transported thousands of miles; and volumes of cheese, yogurt, and electronic products from faraway Finland, France, Greece, Taiwan, and, of course, China.

Let me fill you in on ground transport (trucking), sea transport (containers and bulk cargo), air transport, freight forwarding, and rail transport. These areas will lead in to discussions of the third-party logistics provider; of UPS, FedEx, and DHL; and the important and growing role of China in the logistics and supply chain arena.

Remember that most modes of transport or carriers were "made" in a sense by a product or thing: Old Railway Express by railroad cars, UPS by the truck or delivery van, FedEx by the jet plane, and Maersk Line by the ever-growing containership.

AIR

Airports worldwide handle passengers and cargo in ever-larger quantities. FedEx's Memphis hub ranks the highest in the world in the amount of cargo handled, while Louisville, the main air hub for UPS, ranks 11th.

The International Air Transport Association anticipates that cargo growth between 2005 and 2009 will hover around 6 percent worldwide, with slightly more traffic in Asia and less in Latin America and Africa. Because the establishment of new hubs is already difficult, times ahead may call for far more funding, planning, and execution to make the world's supply chain run smoothly.

The global airfreight business is now growing in the neighborhood of 9 percent per year, which is more than cargo growth and includes ancillary services such as tracking and intermodal services. This business and U.S. domestic airfreight are finally on track to where they were in 2000. Being an airfreight carrier means more than having cargo space on a plane. It most often also means having distribution centers, offices, and hubs that serve to expedite the transportation service as close to the market demands as possible. It requires smart backup of all that hardware and activity with Web-based networks.

SEA

Sea-lanes grew out of trade lanes that were a reflection of trade winds. The fastest route from A to B was rarely a straight line on the map. The big oil tankers, containerships, and other large bulk carriers now ply the seas in ever greater number and move at about 20 to 25 knots. They move most of the world's goods. Containerships are the core of product movement: If all the 200,000,000 containers used in one year were placed end to end, they would circle the Earth. Their needs have called for more and more high technology at ports, and a supporting infrastructure of roads, rail, cranes, piers, terminals, and distribution centers. The limitation of sea trade is not the ships; the latest containership, the *Emma Maersk,* is 1,302 feet long and can carry 11,000 TEU containers at a speed approaching 30 miles per hour. TEU stands for 20-foot equivalent unit and is the standard measure for quantity of containers, as on a containership. A 40-foot container is two TEUs. The problem is in the ports and infrastructure: How do you dock a ship of this size at ports built for smaller ships? How do you on-load efficiently. This is the largest shipbuilding boom of all time, but it is not, in many countries, the boom of port building and infrastructure development and extension. The economics are with the bigger ships, even though they are more expensive. Their presence means, particularly in the United States, higher bridges, longer docks, more modern and larger cranes, more roads, and more rail. For example, the replacement of the Gerald Desmond Bridge in the Port of Los Angeles is slated to cost $800 million.

GROUND

Of the 3.4 million truck drivers on U.S. roads in 2002, about 1.3 million were heavy truck and tractor trailer drivers. About 600,000 new trucks are bought each year. The American Trucking Association (ATA) estimates that employment will increase at a minimum rate of 1.8 percent through to 2012, when there will be a need for 2.1 million heavy haulers. These estimates are cause for alarm in the transportation industry, as there is already a shortage of 20,000 long-haul drivers. Additionally, 219,000 truck drivers will reach retirement age and need to be replaced in the next decade. The pressure increases when we consider this shortage within the context of the industry's explosive growth: In 2005, the total tonnage hauled by trucks was 10.7 billion tons. This figure is expected to rise to 13 billion tons by 2016. Our roads will not serve this load.

By contrast, the number of truck drivers in China is estimated at 900,000. The trucks are almost all nonfleet, and that means small-time mom-and-pop ownership. It is little wonder that trucking is less efficient in China, particularly when combined with less than adequate roads and the arduous customs process. The country's traffic hauling coal is more like idling, which adds to the already problematic pollution.

However, the worst traffic in the United States is getting even worse. We can't throw stones at the Chinese. The traffic pollutes as the vehicles idle. Traffic wastes the time of trucks and passenger cars; the annual delay per driver is in excess of 47 hours per year. It creates delayed shipments. It wastes over 2.3 billion gallons of fuel each year. The cost of U.S. traffic delays is conservatively, according to the Texas Transportation Institute, $63.1 billion a year based on 2003 figures for fuel waste.

ON THE RAILS

Rail in Europe and Japan is infinitely better structured and more efficient than in the United States or China. The United States had a great rail system at one point, but it has not been added to appreciably in the past 30 years. In fact, there are fewer tracks than 30 years ago, and there are now only seven major railroad companies. The problem of rail in the United States is conversion to better intermodal transport. New control technology is now moving into U.S. commercial railroads. Trains can haul material such as coal or concrete, grain, or large liquid containers for longer distances, and less expensively, than trucks. Part of the problem has been the impression by railroaders that they are in the train business, while, in fact, they are in a competitive transportation business. This means that they don't see railroading in the context of other transportation means. They miss the fact that they are competing for traffic with trucks and air.

Having a right of way is a great advantage, as is the use of rails that reduce the friction of hauling. There are other major new advantages. For instance, a double stack freight train is a sight to behold. One train is able to replace as many as 300 trucks. A double stacker is able to achieve nine times the fuel efficiency of highway movement of the same tonnage volume.

The U.S. railroads invested $8 billion in 2006 alone. Railroads are increasing capacity, speed, safety, and efficiency. Unlike highway extension projects that need additional land and may involve large if not bloated costs, prolonged delays that can take years, and increasing public opposition, many rail lines can multiply today's rail capacity. They can do this by adding track on rights-of-way the railroad companies already own. Meanwhile, highway congestion is a growing plague. The public investments being made in highway infrastructure are not relieving congestion. The end result is more traffic and moving the traffic jams to different locations.

THIRD-PARTY LOGISTICS

As business increased and market niches grew, it became easier for specialists in shipping to commandeer some of the business of transportation. Logistics companies consisting of movers, truckers, warehousing facilities, and air and sea services became known as third-party logistics providers (3PLs). They specialized in ocean traffic, rail, road, and, as time went by, airfreight. Between 1965 and 1990, some 3PLs extended their services to customers across all the modes of transportation. The growth of the nascent pull economy was large enough to accommodate not only the 3PLs, but also UPS and its competitors.

The past 20 years have seen a change in the character of 3PLs. They (and their competition—FedEx, DHL, UPS, and the United States Postal Service) have gone from paper-dominated recordkeeping to computer-related applications, bar codes, wireless systems, and the use of the World Wide Web. By these means, they establish the records of procurement and supply, as well as transportation visibility (of everything from a single package to a large load of pallets) as these items move through the pickup and distribution cycle worldwide.

3PL EXAMPLE

SEKO, a third-party freight forwarder, is built on an entrepreneurial base (rather than through wholly owned home office satellites), and the U.S. franchise partners own equity in the company. It has 46 offices in North America and more than 40 worldwide. This means it can serve as a forwarder almost anyplace.

It operates as a group of integrated franchises, and it has taken this same model globally so that it now has strategic partners, and not just agents, all around the world. The franchise partner abroad will eventually see a share of the profits based on the volume of business that is done. Freight forwarders move freight in any manner that they can. They use commercial carriers and integrated airfreight carriers that have fleets of planes.

SEKO is able to do pick (sorting and collecting) and pack work. While other facilities such as their Louisville warehouse facility may have only 100,000 square feet. The company warehouses machines for medical equipment businesses and provides them as needed. This can include specialized delivery and setup at the facility; it may also sterilize the equipment, for instance, before packing and re-storing it.

Third-party logistics providers can act as receivers, storing providers, product assemblers, product refashion providers (as in computer upgrades), product return providers, and distributors. They also help take care of difficult governmental transport regulations such as the United States' Sarbanes-Oxley disclosure regulations; national customs; and new regional regulations, such as the European Union's Registration, Evaluation, Authorization, and Restriction of Chemicals (REACH) directive of 2006.

Logistics and supply chain management are primary organizing concepts within the world of business, and we will see worldwide growth in third-party providers. They will continue to have a major part in what constitutes modern business practice of the supply chain and its logistics functions.

INTRODUCTION TO CARRIER NETWORKS

Commercial carriers companies such as UPS, FedEx, and DHL are large-scale third-party providers. It should be noted that the three large carriers are competitive—in some cases, fiercely so. FedEx dominates air express service, with UPS a strong second; DHL is not a major air player in the sense that it doesn't own its own aircraft. On the ground, UPS is somewhere around five times the size of FedEx, delivering about 15 million packages a day. Another major differentiator between UPS and FedEx is that UPS is unionized, while FedEx runs on an owner/operator model. UPS and FedEx are U.S. companies and have the advantage over DHL in the United States because DHL is a German company and has some restrictions as to how it does business in the United States.

As carriers redefine from being package delivery companies to being global commerce companies, their collaboration will increase. Some collaborations will end in mergers; UPS, for example, has acquired many companies in the past 10 years: Challenge Air Cargo, Fritz Companies, Inc., First International Bancorp, and recently Menlo Worldwide Forwarding. DHL was acquired by Deutsche Post World Net in 2002; it has also made strategic alliances with Lufthansa, Japan Airlines, and the Chinese government. FedEx in turn acquired Parcel Direct and Kinko's in 2004.

Let me trace the commercial carrier story from its origin. UPS dominated the industry until 1969, when DHL was established; FedEx joined the game two years later. The period of time between 1968 and 1973 is filled with interesting advances. The computer mouse was born in 1968, and hypertext the following year, bringing about a dramatic change in manufacturing opportunity with the invention of the programmable logic controller (a kind of manufacturing control computer). ARPANET (the preliminary system that became the Internet) was operating, the microprocessor was born, and the first cell phone was invented. These developments laid the groundwork for the scale and speed of freight today.

CASEY AT THE BAT

Jim Casey, the founder of UPS, started his business in 1907. He founded the company by borrowing $100 from a friend to start the American Messenger Company in Seattle in 1907.

Six year earlier, two men in Milwaukee had taken out a loan of $1,000 to start Allen-Bradley, a business that would create controls that would later be essential to automated sorting systems that expedited warehousing and distribution centers for UPS. At first, the American Messenger Company was Jim Casey on his bicycle delivering local Seattle messages. This was an entrepreneur well on his way.

Unlike later competitors, the Post Office Department, as it was first called, could not accomplish fast door-to-door delivery. It had drop boxes and, over time, rural post offices, where mail and packages could be taken, but it did not pick up packages at stores and businesses. Mail in the United States was delivered by train beginning in 1829 in Pennsylvania; a hundred years later, 10,000 trains were moving the mail. The United States Postal Service did experiment with using government planes for airmail, but by 1927, it had shifted airmail to commercial carriers.

STORE-TO-HOME DELIVERY

Established Seattle retailers such as Wallin & Nordstrom, and emerging stores such as The Bon Marché, The Rhodes Company, and Fraser Paterson, became the core of Casey's store-to-home delivery service. He and his employees had found their niche, and it was a good one.

The way to success was mergers and takeovers. It was thus for Casey who with his brother George merged with McCabe's Motorcycle Messengers. Merchants Parcel Delivery bought a Model T with which to deliver store packages. Casey came up with the fundamental innovative idea that each truck would deliver to only a single geographical area in the city. It was a simple but effective "logistics" decision. The company expanded to Oakland, California, and by 1919, began to use the name United Parcel Service. The Model T vans multiplied and were configured with large rear storage boxes that have changed very little over the years. The rear storage boxes were tall for two innovative reasons: a driver could work easily standing up, and it allowed for two shelves of packages and the beginnings of a several-shelves-high sorting system.

In 1922, the United Parcel Service moved its central offices to Los Angeles. The move reinforced the open-mindedness of Casey and his crew: They were willing to go where the opportunity was. The company installed its first conveyor belt system in 1924, turning a garage into a distribution center before the term had been coined. The conveyor system used mechanical technology to reinforce Casey's original idea of specific loads for specific trucks for specific delivery. Packages would come in from stores on one side, and be sorted by location and sent out by truck on the other side. This idea would later bloom into UPS managed distribution centers globally. In all cases, the centers were placed as close as possible to the locations for pickup and delivery.

DELIVERY HEAVEN

In 1930, the opportunity to deliver for three large retail stores in Manhattan persuaded the company to relocate to New York City. New York also had in its five boroughs millions of homes that needed delivery service from stores. UPS expanded from its New York base to cities along the East Coast. World War II served as a large-scale logistics model for some of the more perceptive in commerce.

UPS had started United Air Express in 1929, but shut down air services two years later due to the slow economy. After the war, however, the Berlin airlift proved that massive supplies could be delivered quickly by air. United Parcel Service renewed its air business in 1953 with two-day service from the West Coast to East Coast cities using other carrier planes.

BOOMS

A major change in demographics occurred as the baby boom came to pass. It led to the amazing suburban growth of America. GIs and families moved in far greater numbers to houses in the suburbs. They bought products from city stores, as the shopping mall had yet come into being. Suburban sprawl brought a great challenge to all carriers. A city-dominated company like UPS had to go to suburbia—and it did. When the mall explosion happened in the 1960s, UPS switched gears and delivered from mall stores to local homes. The challenges for UPS in the 1970s and 1980s came from greatly increased competition, and this meant reexamination from top to bottom of their business.

DHL went into business in 1969, with FedEx close on its heels in 1971, and in 1970, the United States Postal Service introduced an experimental overnight express service. The threat of competition induced UPS to reinvent itself and go for more innovation, including delivery to and from individual customers and companies outside of retailing. This required strategically located distribution centers and offices nationwide, each with all the equipment and support structure necessary to function. The UPS mission shifted gradually from delivery as a core to customer solutions. These carriers were in at the "invention" of customer-driven businesses.

While this ground activity took place nationally, and, in time, internationally, UPS started building what would become the world's ninth largest airline. Investing in airfreight was a sound business decision because FedEx was establishing its air service and would in time become the largest airfreight cargo handler in the world. (FedEx had from its origin made air transport its distinguishing feature; it remains the largest commercial cargo carrier and still sees its principal role as an air express service.) Airport hubs and aircraft brought these companies into freight forwarding of bulk goods (palletized packages). The complexities of freight forwarding meant that they had to learn all the tricks of intermodal transportation (truck to air, air to truck, truck to sea and rail). They had to accomplish this against a background of increasingly competing services, such as a massive number of smaller-scale freight forwarders that acted as third-party transportation providers.

USPS

While DHL and FedEx gained footholds in the industry, the United States Postal Service continued to increase its delivery volume through the late 1980s. By 1982, optical character readers were reading the addresses on mail and adding bar codes for delivery. In 1983, the USPS introduced four-digit extensions to the existing five-digit ZIP code, allowing for faster sorting and targeted delivery. This became the means of businesses sorting their own targeted business and customers.

The USPS had 780,000 employees at its peak, and by 1983, it was expected to operate without public subsidy. With nearly 40,000 post offices, it delivered almost half of the world's mail. Today it delivers 212 billion pieces of mail to over 144 million homes, businesses, and post office boxes each year—about 44 percent of the world's mail, with annual revenue of around $70 billion.

DHL ARRIVES

In its early years, the most notable difference between DHL and UPS or FedEx was that DHL almost immediately went international. Its expansion started in 1971, and had gone as far as a presence in Japan and parts of the Pacific by 1972 and an early presence in Europe, in the U.K. in 1974, and in Germany by 1977. Today it is a German company, owned by Deutsche Post World Net of Bonn, Germany, and Plantation, Florida.

Today DHL has services in over 220 countries, operates 4,000 offices, and reaches 12,000 destinations. It has 170,000 employees, and is growing. It operates 420 aircraft. Its global system includes 238 gateways and 450 hubs, warehouses, and terminals that serve over 4 million customers worldwide. Its shipments are in excess of 1.5 billion a year. It introduced document delivery service to Japan, Hong Kong, and Singapore as early as 1972, and, by 1979, offered package delivery as well.

DHL INNOVATIONS

DHL's early move to a world trade posture was, and probably still is, its major innovation. This strategy brought it to a strong presence in China, where it still dominates on-the-ground delivery—well ahead of the game. Its innovations often take on the color of, or the nature of, the country within which it is operating: It uses canal barges in Europe and street carts in the urban activity centers of New York City.

It has in recent years become more like its counterparts UPS and FedEx in the breadth of its business and in scale of the bulk goods and packages transported.

GOLDEN LINK

As DHL was making moves overseas, UPS had a series of battles with the Federal Trade Commission and the U.S. government in the period between 1950 and 1975. It won the opportunity to offer its services in all the states of the Union, referred to in the company as the "golden link." This meant that UPS could pick up and deliver from anywhere in the United States and deliver to any home address in the United States and, soon after, Canada. FedEx, after years of similar lobbying got Public Law 95-163 passed, allowing cargo airlines to fly without route restrictions and in larger and more economical freight airplaner.

FEDEX MAKES ITS ENTRANCE

The Federal Express Corporation was founded in Little Rock, Arkansas, in 1971, 65 years after UPS. It didn't compete directly with UPS so much as it created its own business: airfreight and overnight delivery. In 1973, the company moved to Memphis when Little Rock hedged providing air facilities for it. FedEx first connected 25 U.S. cities using Dassault Falcon jets, which were fast but did not have sufficient capacity. Therefore, in 1977, FedEx purchased seven Boeing 727s. The FedEx way was, and still is, a combination of vehicles and computer technology and its related digital communication. In 1979, it developed COSMOS, a computer system that integrates people, packages, and vehicles.

Memphis International Airport has become, with the presence of FedEx, the airport with the greatest volume of air cargo handling in the world on a throughput reading (throughput refers to loads being transferred in and out, rather than merely what is unloaded at the site). FedEx had $29.4 billion in sales in 2005 organized around 899 express stations as operating facilities. Its airfreight service centers number 321, while it has 10 air hubs allowing for the operation of 677 aircraft. These aircraft serve 375 airports and are backed up by 29 ground hubs and a ground fleet of 70,000 vehicles. The company's 260,000 employees offer services in 220 countries. FedEx delivers and picks up at all U.S. addresses. Its average daily volume amounts to six million express, ground, freight, and extended services deliveries.

The FedEx overnight letter was an innovation that depended on air service, as does the next-day letter (you are not going to make it across country on a horse). FedEx also pioneered time-definite freight that added further dependability to its service. Its move to Europe and Asia came in 1984, and to Japan in 1988. The concentration on FedEx Air Freight was, in the context of the time, an innovation.

Each of these major carriers has its shining service: UPS on the ground, FedEx in the air, and DHL in international services. There are other carriers such as Airborne, Purolator, and Emery, and they each play their own role.

GOING INTERNATIONAL

Global trade is one more indication of the changeover from a push generation to a pull generation. Doing business globally means satisfying ever more closely the demands of the customer (by price, quality, and inventiveness). DHL is a good example of this, as meanwhile in the 1970s, it was opening up offices in London and Frankfort, and, soon after, offering service in the Middle East and Africa. By 1979, DHL was delivering packages as well as its established document delivery. The success of these FTC-approved operations led UPS to establish overseas services, starting in Germany.

By 1988, UPS had built a base of operations with its air service in 49 countries; over time, it would connect to every major country in the world. These services meant having hubs and offices in the countries served; having linkage to their computer systems in order to track and process orders, transportation schedules, custom forms, and bills of lading; and acting as language service providers, packagers, sorters, and carrier service. The service today is extended to over 200 countries and territories.

By the mid-1980s, computer systems had become more robust and larger in memory, and applications were available that made the sorting of data in databases a fundamental part of transportation and goods management. As wireless technology took hold, each commercial carrier driver, flier, or supervisor could use a computer or handheld device, along with bar code, to keep track of the mountains of data moving millions of packages a day. UPS's Worldport distribution center processes 304,000 packages an hour—that means 84 packages each a second.

DISTRIBUTION CENTERS LINKED TO TRAFFIC

As UPS, FedEx, and DHL (and, of course, other carriers such as USPS, Purolator, and many, many other 3PLs) grew, their methods of storing and sorting grew with them. They found the heavy traffic zones and built offices and distribution centers as nearby as possible. These services became linked by EDI and phone first, and are now connected by Web-based networks that allow all personnel to access the information for which they are authorized and responsible. This means hundreds of thousands of people at thousands of locations.

United Parcel Service is now headquartered in Atlanta, Georgia, and had revenue of $42.6 billion in 2005. Its employees number 407,200, of which 58,000 are outside the United States. The company's delivery volume amounts to 3.75 billion packages and documents a year, or about 14.8 million packages and documents each day, with a service area of more than 200 countries and territories. It uses a delivery fleet of 91,700 package vehicles and 268 planes, making its air fleet the ninth largest in the world.

That goes to prove the need for exabytes and all that information: It has to be immediately available to thousands of workers and customers all over the world and often at the same time.

Today UPS has over 400,000 employees; FedEx has 250,000, DHL has over 200,000, and the USPS has over 700,000. This is a lot of people working to deliver mail, documents, and packages. The push economy had given way to the pull economy and these people essentially are in business to make sure that their clients can pick up and deliver what a customer wants, when and where a customer wants it. They are, along with hundreds of other third-party logistics providers, the enablers of meeting customer demand from many to one.

TRACKING

The carriers focused on distribution and tracking methodology. Bar codes had been used for decades, but with each decade, the system became more robust and less difficult to use, gradually extending its technology, as in scanning at greater distances. The carriers (along with other leaders such as Dell in manufacturing and Wal-Mart in retailing) understood the strategic importance of hubs and distribution centers equipped with this new technology, and with modern forklifts, portable communication, and computing.

In another innovative move, UPS took over a majority of Mail Boxes Etc. stores and converted them to 4,000 franchise-operated pickup, pack, and delivery centers. They added to these 40,000 strategically located drop boxes. DHL had street couriers delivering by cart—and, with their handheld computers, doing so most effectively. This is a great example of reaching customers where they live. Not to be outdone, FedEx acquired Kinko's 1,200 stores devoted to business processing. The new venture became FedEx Kinko's Office and Print Services and a place to print, package, and deliver.

Carriers, manufacturers, and retailers will now have an opportunity to take radio frequency identification (RFID) to the next step. Advanced RFID will be one aspect of mobile computing and communicating. The inlays that act as tiny computers in present-day RFID tags will become full-line computers with communication capability and with a surround of sensors that provide whatever information the tag is designed to give. If the tag is attached to a perishable food item, it might give temperature information or warning. If the product is an electronic part, the sensors could communicate to the computer inlay and describe if it had been dropped or damaged.

These kinds of RFID tags will revolutionize warehouses, transport delivery, retail, and the market. Each package, each letter, each pallet will be assigned by RFID technology to the level of intelligence that is required to do the job. This is adaptive and distributed technology in a nutshell with increased visibility. Carriers have developed supply chain solutions that take on the integration of sales, marketing, finance, and technology resources for supply chain subsidiaries. This effort is a confirmation of their total move from a push economy to a pull economy, from a delivery service to a business solutions service.

CARRIERS ON THE WEB

The technology of Web-based business was not invented or really innovated by the carriers (DHL, FedEx, UPS, or other 3PLs), but it caught on rapidly and has benefited the industry in terms of efficiency, cost, and customer satisfaction. FedEx's website went live in 1994, allowing some of its customers the opportunity to conduct business on the Internet. Lawrence Roberts, one of the principal developers of Internet technology, was the president and CEO of DHL in 1982, a formative year in the Internet's creation. UPS offered tracking of ground shipments via the Web in 1992, and via mobile cellular service a year later. By the year 2000, the UPS site handled 6.5 million online tracking requests per day. This service, in time, allowed UPS to deliver over 14 million packages daily, with the ready option of customer tracking on all those deliveries. In 2002, the company began offering online returns service. Given that a great deal of the company's business is with other businesses (and still with stores), the Web becomes a vital link within those businesses and stores. It is their ticket to knowing what is where and when.

FedEx, UPS, and DHL are very much aware that their success is tied to communication. That means being networked, operating in real time, and communicating and responding digitally. Competitors in the form of other smaller 3PLs are now offering much the same services although only rarely on the global scale of the big three.

CHALLENGES TO CARRIERS

The carriers did not have to invent *things* so much as *services*. For example, they didn't invent the truck engine or the disk drive. They invented services such as next-day delivery, air express, convenient customer tracking of their goods, and the use of bar codes in sorting on a large scale. They use and refine hand-held computers and packaging modules.

After 9/11, identification and security became a larger issue with carriers and all those involved in commerce. Identification and tracking link, to some extent, to security as well. U.S. government regulations in drugs and health care had before 9/11 created sets of compliance rules for tracking and safeguarding the distribution and use of these products. In today's security atmosphere, all packages are suspect until proven innocent—a reversal of our normal legal process

IT'S THE CUSTOMER

Customers today have choices, and they no longer expect to simply have their packages delivered. They expect carriers to extend themselves by offering new services—for example, warehousing, remanufacture, or returns management. Remanufacture can mean anything from a simple upgrade of a product all the way to a full redesign and manufacture of a product for a customer. Returns management is a process that receives the returned goods by an established procedure, exchanges the goods, repairs or remanufactures the goods, and then repackages them and sends them back to the customer with all attendant financial work as part of the process. All carriers, including the vast number of 3PLs, have a multitude of customers; that's the heart of their business. For instance, UPS has 7.9 million customers per day, which translates into 3.75 billion packages and documents per year. It receives 10 million online requests for tracking per day. In order to accomplish these services, UPS utilizes 15 mainframes, 2,342 mid-range computers, 8,700 servers, and 149,000 LAN workstations.

In 2003, FedEx teamed up with Amazon.com to act as the delivery service for *Harry Potter and the Order of the Phoenix;* on the day of its release this amounted to the delivery of 400,000 copies in one day. This is the epitome of delivering successfully to one customer at a time en masse. It further reached its customers through its acquisition of 1,200 Kinko's stores. This puts FedEx right in the face of those who need delivery services.

DHL customers have traditionally been international. The company's spread from the West Coast of the United States to world customers was augmented when it was acquired by Deutsche Post, a German company with a global proclivity. DHL also reaches out to customers in embattled areas such as Iraq and Burma, and is the only courier that delivers to Cuba and North Korea.

THE CHINA CARD

The center of growth in the supply chain is China, or, in a slightly larger view, the Asia-Pacific region. Big commercial carriers, as well as companies such as IBM (which has moved its world procurement headquarters to Shenzhen, China), Wal-Mart, Dell, Hewlett-Packard, GE, and many more are now seeing China as the playing field. China is the fastest growing economy in the world, followed by India.

UPS's Asia-Pacific service area, headquartered in Singapore, serves more than 40 countries and 330 cities in China. UPS has 6,500 employees in the Asia-Pacific and 4,000 in China alone. The airports it serves are Taipei, Taiwan, Hong Kong, Singapore, and Pampanga in the Philippines.

UPS reached out to China as new market before most other businesses, but DHL had been there previously. Since 2000, UPS has created distribution centers, air hubs, and truck fleets for the China trade that is booming. UPS today sees China (and Asia) as a major business front, probably its most important in regard to growth; the company is making enormous financial investments in hubs, people, and equipment in Asia.

FedEx established its express operations in China in 1984 and added freight operations in 1995. Its China region headquarters is Shanghai and from there it serves more than 220 countries and territories. It also serves 200 domestic cities with more than 300 employees in China, picking up from 100 drop-off locations.

DHL's infrastructure in China is complemented by a dedicated air network in the region, currently comprising 27 destinations, which is served by more than 20 aircraft in dedicated freighter operations. In addition, DHL utilizes more than 500 commercial flights every week in China. DHL also has strategic direct flights linking key cities in China with the international marketplace. The company currently offers around 5,000 drop points across the Asia-Pacific region available through its service centers, express centers, and retail outlets, as well as through partnerships with third-party retailers and resellers.

SUMMING UP: TRANSPORT BY GROUND, AIR, SEA, AND RAIL

The development of logistics, as in the case of carriers and all they stand for in strategies, planning, execution, places, and equipment, has been a reflection of local companies expanding in several ways. They expanded into a wider geographical sphere, and into the use and refinement of transportation, communication, and computing capabilities. They learned to work with suppliers and retailers worldwide. They formed advantageous partnerships. They saw and responded to the shift from a push strategy to a pull strategy, and they embraced the supply chain as it became evident in their world.

Chapter 10

PINS TO PORSCHES: THE EVOLUTION OF MANUFACTURING

Making things is as old as humankind. It is our nature and defines us like our thumbs, our larger brains, and the nature of our voice boxes. It is a defining difference. Woven goods, nets, clothing, pottery, and weapons such as clubs, swords, knives, and spears in metal and wood evolved over hundreds of thousands of years. Almost all were the products of craftsmen or groups of craftsmen working side by side. Labor was intensely directed to making a complete object as in making a nail, or a pot, or a wheel—one person, one pin; one person, one pot; and so on. People worked in this way for hundreds of years.

Adam Smith changed manufacturing when he wrote *The Wealth of Nations* in 1776. He described a process of manufacture that separated tasks, even when making a lowly pin. He "invented" the division of labor. Its advantages included more production and less-skilled workers, and therefore more profit. This was in some ways the beginning of logistics and the supply chain.

WHITNEY AND INTERCHANGEABLE PARTS

To this mix was soon added the work of Eli Whitney (known best for the cotton gin), whose work in interchangeable parts in muskets and clocks changed musket manufacture, and manufacturing generally, in a fundamental way. The interchangeable part made mass manufacture possible to a great extent, as parts were not craft fashioned but held to the rigid repeatability of being manufactured automatically by machine or semi-automatically. Each part became like the next part in a manufactured sequence and could be used interchangeably in a product such as a gun. Europe had had success with interchangeable parts (muskets in France and Navy pulley blocks in England) before Whitney. The difference was that developing New England embraced the principle as a necessity for most manufacturing, whereas Europe saw interchangeability as an exception to the normal means of manufacture.

On the other side of the world there were pulley blocks before there was a pull strategy. The first integrated factory line was implemented around 1790. In order to do this, 45 machines were built, each of which was designed to accomplish a single step in the manufacturing process. The 130,000 pulley blocks the Royal Navy needed each year were so manufactured. The clock and mass production changed the world's economy, its manufacture, and, in time, its supply chains and logistics.

AMERICAN SYSTEM OF MANUFACTURING

American manufacturing was unique in many ways: an emphasis on organization, the use of plentiful resources (such as waterpower, open land, minerals, coal), and the employment of plentiful but unskilled labor. Most factories chose to make the machinery specialized in its processes, not the worker. The Boston Manufacturing Company did just this, creating factories whose principle was intelligent logistical passing of goods (in this case cotton cloth) from one process to another and from one end of the factory to the other. This constituted an invention of organization and integration. The real American contribution was not an invention of machines, but a new way of organizing work.

AGE OF ELECTRICITY AND EFFICIENCY

The turn of the 20th century, and immediately after, was the age of mechanical and electrical discovery, particularly in the United States—an age dominated by Thomas Edison, Alexander Graham Bell, the Wright brothers, and Henry Ford. The stringing of telephone poles and cables transformed city and town streets, and soon, railed trolleys with their overhead electric cables helped further the transformation. Big cities such as New York had already committed to subways by 1904. The telephone took the speed and ease of communication far beyond the telegraph.

Mechanical progress had another side, and that was the human equation in the production of goods. A movement spearheaded by Frederick W. Taylor examined the efficiency of the physical processes of work. Taylor's book *The Principles of Scientific Management*, published in 1911, studied stopwatch timing of work, intense observation of the sequence of work, and the interrelationship between a worker and his or her tools.

By analyzing the process of work, Taylor not only made it more efficient, but unknowingly set up work for eventual automation. By looking at work systematically, he also anticipated logistics as now practiced and the supply chain as it became a realizable system.

FROM PIGS TO MUSTANGS

The meat packing industry was the forerunner of the modern automobile manufacturing plant. Meat processing in Chicago invented the overhead railway and the systematic provision of actions coordinated with the presence of livestock and meat at various levels of processing. The meat processing industry also made use of complex packaging techniques first used in England, as in tinning meat. Chicago took it to a new level by coordinating the huge stockyards; the carts and eventually trucks to the processing plants; the killing of the animals; the butchering, sorting, and use of all the parts; and their packaging or transfer as sides of beef or pork to refrigeration (ice houses) and subsequent distribution to stores, restaurants, and wholesalers. The yards introduced overhead conveyers as a means to move the animals and their parts, and this technique was picked up by the automotive manufacturers. The yards created sectional processing as in skinning and sectioning the animal parts. This same sectioning of functions became the norm in automotive production as well. Chicago invented fast processing in a way the world had never seen; it was only a matter of time before this spread to other manufacturers and to distribution systems and warehousing. The precursor of UPS's Worldport is the processing of pigs near the stockyard; out of the reeking stockyards of Chicago comes a big part of the modern world of freight and mail processing.

THE AMERICAN MASS PRODUCTION SYSTEM

The American production system, as it came to be known by the world, was essentially a mass production system as practiced by Ford with his Model T, first produced in 1909. This was a business system now seen as a push strategy. This meant manufacturing and marketing as many products as possible of a certain quality, with the only restraint being the plant's or factory's capacity. Goods were pushed out to the wholesaler, retailer, and customer. Those that did not sell were held in warehouses or on dealer car lots. The general effect of this was both positive and negative. There was always a car for a buyer, but the car might well be not a car of his or her choice. In a push strategy, the manufacturer makes the choices; while in a later push economy, the choices are customer driven.

Those days, of course, are gone. The strategy now is to manufacture, distribute, and retail by demand.

A "LET'S DO IT" PUSH ECONOMY

Peace changed the business of World War II to a business of factory conversion and a flood of new and reissued consumer goods: TVs, cars, washing machines, refrigerators, and radios. The dominance of U.S. manufacturing over other countries came about for several reasons: available manpower, available land, and inventors and innovators. The push economy had started its juggernaut development in the years before World War II as the nations came out of the Great Depression. But its real impact was not seen until after 1945.

The push system was basically mass production combined with an early Ford version of just-in-time technique and a ready market of buyers. The roots of complex logistics and the supply chain, therefore, began in the period between 1900 and 1950. These developments were followed rapidly by the advent of the supermarket, the mall, and eventually the early Wal-Mart, whose first store opened in 1962 in Rogers, Arkansas. There would not have been a need for these, if it had not been for the mass production capability of U.S. manufacturing. Goods poured out, and goods had to be shipped and sold. U.S. manufacturing was revolutionized again by the work of W. Edwards Deming, a statistician who first studied manufacturing in the 1920s. He saw the manufacturing process as a passing along from one person or task to another, and within each step, value was added. He described this process in August 1950 as, "production viewed as system" anticipating by more than 30 years the advent of the supply chain. Deming saw the chain as moving from supplier to manufacturer to distributor. He saw all the essential parts, but never went as far as creating the supply chain as such.

PUSH STAGGERS

The world was changing, and business was changing along with it. International trade was increasing. The advent of the profitable DC-3 brought about a surge in aircraft design intended for both passenger and freight hauling. The infrastructure had to follow the development and manufacture of planes. The airports of the 1950s, 1960s, and even later were awkward for freight, because freight was, to an extent, an afterthought. Regardless, UPS jumped in with airfreight service in 1953. The planes themselves were fine, but the handling of freight was at best crude. The pioneers persisted and newcomers such as FedEx prospered to a great extent (though not until the 1970s) because of their airfreight capability.

PUSH TO PULL

Once people had the basics from out of the mass production cornucopia they started to get selective and expected new models and new products yearly, and, soon, even more often. A pull strategy in manufacturing turned from concerns of how many to how good, how new, and how quickly available.

A real pull strategy is about the execution of the opportunities systems have to offer. The dividing of the effective company from the less effective company is most often in its process execution. It is about minimum use of trucks, planes, sea carriers, and rail and minimal intermodal transfers. The question has to be asked, is this process necessary (as in a warehouse transfer)? Does it take the business closer to the customer, and make the process better? It is easy to use more processes or materials, and hard to use less. Pull is about identifying exceptions in an order (this may be identifying a subset of an order that needs either special handling or separate delivery, and that can mean a more satisfied customer) and by gaining opportunities through real-time visibility of process. It might be possible, given real-time information, to deliver a day early and win over a customer and increase profit.

The gradual transfer from a push economy to a pull economy made the nature of warehousing change dramatically. Storage of goods was a cost, while the transfer of goods quickly sorted can be an asset; so there has been a shift away from storing goods unless absolutely necessary, as in emergency situations. The net effect of this is not just less storage, but also less cost for those who can both provide and execute the solution. UPS, Dell, and Wal-Mart have become highly competent practitioners of this shift. The shift is toward mobility and fluidity, and systems that fit this description have no room for storage racks.

PULLING CONCEPTS

Customer demand drives an enterprise's pull strategy for a global business advantage. A pull strategy is at the core of manufacturing, commerce, and retailing. Pull strategy adoption has changed and will continue to change the global economy. Pull cycles start with demand and end with fulfilling demand.

There were several major contributors in the transfer from push to pull. Feedback and automation are key principles in the changeover. Norbert Wiener created the idea of feedback in its modern sense. The behavior of a tool, machine, or process could be regulated by feedback principles through electrical and eventually electronic means. Processes could therefore become self-regulating, as with a thermostat. This set in motion the principles that made possible robotics, automation, and the creation of sensors.

Automation certainly existed before John Diebold spread the word; it just didn't have a name. Diebold made one very significant contribution to the use. He expanded the context of the word to include not only mechanical processes, but also computing and the processing of information. This link changed a great deal of the way we work in today's business, and expedited a pull economy. It has been the automation of information, more than robots or automatic machine tools that has transformed our world. Even in manufacturing, it is the integration of information through the use of computers that has changed manufacturing. Information automation has spread out of the factory and into business and commerce at large. Information affects finishing, packaging, design, engineering, marketing, and sales, and is nowhere more forceful than in the financial domain. Diebold's real contribution was not the word *automation* but the concept of automation as a principle integral to information processing. Automated information would control automated machine processing and expedite data processing.

TOYOTA PRODUCTION SYSTEM

The emergence within Japan in the 1970s of the Toyota Production System was a full expression of the new pull strategy, and is still the strongest manufacturing strategy for meeting a customer's on-demand needs.

The context of the system is one of process stability. This stability has to be extended through a range of basic system elements: environment, people, methodologies, the materials used, and the machines that are applicable. The Toyota Production System has two pillars: J-I-T and *jidoka*, which in combination are very powerful. J-I-T is supply chain oriented, fully as it is a strategy that concentrates on moving things on time and at the highest level of performance. Jidoka is a combination of highest quality in each manufacturing and distribution step, and the management of exceptions or irregularities. Toyota has made the system into an "engine" that delivers not just great products but also—as with any well-oiled supply chain system—charmed and satisfied customers. Many manufacturers all over the world are now following and improving this process.

FROM SILOS TO BACKBONES

Traditional manufacturing inherited a clumsy set of methods from its root structure that included "silos" between design, engineering, manufacturing, and finishing and packaging, marketing, and sales. Silos are departmental systems or structures that inherently separate the workflow of the company as a whole. The development of computer integrated manufacturing (CIM) favored getting rid of the walls between functions. CIM as a strategy connects separate tools, processes, workstations, and manufacturing lines by computer control using software that integrates the steps and timing of manufacturing. It grew up alongside what was called manufacturing resource planning (MRP) that evolved to Enterprise Resource Planning (ERP) and now is the backbone of an enterprise's extended manufacturing presence and practice.

ENTERPRISE RESOURCE PLANNING

As the supply chain developed in concert with logistics, ERP became the connecting network for business. As the Internet came into play, all these forces were joined into networks that allowed for an Internet-enabled supply chain and a digital record that could be compiled in one database. This database of information could be accessed from distant locations by suppliers, shippers, manufacturers, and retailers. This is the world that commerce providers thrive within and help produce. Other software and architectures are augmenting and, to an extent, replacing ERP, but it is still the bedrock of those companies that have adopted it.

PROCESS ENHANCED

Logistics and the supply chain are now becoming the advanced "troops" of business. They are the engines that are leading successful businesses to greater advantage in their market positions and in transactions with their customers. A global trade and global outsourcing of manufacturing and distribution have made logistics and the supply chain vital core tools.

Unlike electronic messages, the movement of goods with dimensions and weight requires a whole other means of delivery. Goods cannot be digitized. They must be moved physically, and this is the impetus for modern pickup and delivery systems. They still extensively use human muscles, carts, motorized lifts, and pallets.

PULLING

Demand (pull) starts with the customer. Many manufacturers now make to order, or come as close to this as possible, and production can now entail the production and distribution of a single item. The demand-driven and synchronized supply chain is custom made for the aggressive business philosophy of today and tomorrow. Logistics and supply chain management are essential organizing sets of techniques and concepts within the world of business. They will continue to have a major part in what constitutes modern business practice. Companies such as IBM, Dell, UPS, FedEx, Wal-Mart, and IKEA apply a demand methodology to their business practice using innovation, demand management, and enhanced processes as up front and very competitive tools.

GREEN INK

The supply chain used to be red ink to business. It was a necessary evil, and there was much cost in dead storage. The supply chain is now seen as a strategic advantage when practiced well. In fact, IBM and a host of other successful companies see logistics and the supply chain as the core means of competition in the 21st century. UPS and its competition have made this turn to the supply chain a very good and profitable global business. They try to position the shipping and handling needs of their customers as if they were on the front lines of their customers' businesses.

The 20th century invented the idea of the customer (and subsequently the demand-driven customer supply chain). Customers are fickle. They change their buying habits. They want options. Rather than simply wanting an item, they want better treatment, and they want things delivered on time and in good condition. The warehouse full of last year's product that had no market became a large liability. The lack of sources for a new product became a major business problem. The coordination of logistics now took a turn toward information systems, EDI, faxing, and dedicated phones. The companies that succeeded were those that saw the customer as the driving force of their supply chains.

DEATH OF PUSH

Push as a vibrant economic force had died. Yet it has taken pull from the mid-1980s until today to see fruition, and it is still on the march. There were many false starts. It was assumed, for instance, that more automation would be enough to create a miracle-like manufacturing base, and many of the same attitudes persisted in commerce and retailing. To be a miracle within manufacturing, a pull methodology would have to be able to either anticipate demand or come close enough in its predictions to make the flow of manufacturing meet the demand of the market precisely enough to maintain company profit. However, more automation applied to a business process can be expensive and unproductive. Certain technologies such as bar coding could be applied easily and cheaply and may have had a greater impact than other more complex solutions to automation.

In the late 1980s through the 1990s, more was going on. Software development for commerce and other business processes were expensive, often overdesigned, and too often not compatible with existing systems. Tools of one generation had to be upgraded to work with electronic information systems of another generation. Turning from one form of economy to another was time consuming and often costly. Those who made good choices persisted all the way to profit.

SUPPLY AS STRATEGIC

Henry Ford had a supplier give him bolts in a specially designed box. The supplier later found that the box was broken down intelligently and later became a Model T body frame. Ford gave a supplier one order and used the results to expedite and lower the cost of manufacturing.

In the Middle Ages, the Crusades failed not for lack of valor but because of overtaxed supply chains. It happened later to Napoleon, and to Hitler. The more extended the supply chain, the better and more robust it must be. If you wish to start a war, start with the supply chain and not with the guns. Manufacturing is not all machinery but rather the means of judging who needs what products and getting them there successfully, and to a single customer if that is what works. Manufacturing may be an organically evolving means by which our societies create what we need from available materials. It is less and less tools and more and more information, more and more processes working in time.

SUMMING UP: PINS TO PORSCHES

Modern manufacturing started with a combination of division of labor and steam energy. It proceeded by leaps and bounds through the industrial revolution, on to the American production system and its mass production. At the end of World War II, it gradually shifted from a push strategy to a pull strategy and from final quality checks to building quality in from the beginning. Toyota implemented J-I-T as a means of production and distribution. Maturing manufacturing became demand driven; to accomplish this, computers and manufacturing software enhanced their control, tracking, and the efficiency and quality of both. If you want to change manufacturing in an age of pull, don't look upon the donut but look upon the hole in its center. It seems it is not what you add to the mix but what you take away.

Chapter

11

ACTIVITY NOT PLACE: OUTSOURCING

Manufacturing used to be associated with a place: a building, a set of factories, and a factory town. Those days are long past.

A factory today is an idea more than a thing. Manufacturing didn't start in buildings as such. It probably started in back alleys, commercial store areas, and bazaars. It was extended craft. It soon came to be localized in buildings, just as one of its prototypes, the blacksmith's shop, was. British and early New England factories very quickly took on a form of being two storied, brick, and with chimneys for the furnaces and the steam engines. A manufacturing establishment became primarily the building it operated within. Building ownership was a core ingredient of the manufacturing enterprise and the factory town became its context, its milieu with factory homes (of sorts), factory stores, factory meeting halls, recreation facilities, and even schools. The factory was the town *and* the town was the factory. They depended on each other.

In the Japanese model after World War II, each surviving apartment became a factory. The big companies in the United States, on the other hand, got into the model of distributed manufacturing that was the first stage of multinational manufacturing. Distributed manufacturing was exemplified by moving automotive manufacturing from Detroit to other locations that provided a labor pool or tax advantage, such as another state. Big corporations easily enlarged this trend to extend their markets, use cheaper labor, and take advantage of local resources overseas; then multinational manufacturing was born. Outsourced manufacturing appears to be a stepchild of multinational manufacturing, which was initially the province of the automotive and computer industries. Things and objects have become subservient to processes; to put it another way, control of process is more important than the location where the process takes place.

This was all before contracted manufacturing and outsourcing really took hold. When most people talk of outsourcing, they refer to the process of sending manufacturing overseas to a place where there is cheap labor. This is by no means the full case.

OUTSOURCING COMES OUT

The word *outsourcing* began to be used around 1982, and is often used loosely. There is a difference between outsourcing and off-shoring. Outsourcing can be taking a part of your business across the street, as in printing, or welding, or telephone service; it refers to the reduction of costs and transfer of the risks of a defined process to a third party. Off-shoring means what it says, that is to take business over the seas, or at least across borders.

One of the first industries to use outsourcing extensively was the publishing industry. Beginning in the 1960s, publishers sent printing to Italy and Spain, where it was significantly less expensive, followed by massive moves in the 1990s to Asia. The other big outsourcing move came through the need for such things as answering services for large corporations, which was fulfilled in India. Since the 1980s, companies in Mexico have specialized in taking in materials from outside, and then manufacturing and distributing them. They have been heavily involved in U.S. automotive manufacture. The information technology sector has done a great deal of outsourcing in recent years, seeking programming expertise in places such as Ireland and with cost advantage in India.

Outsourcing is not really new. But we perceive it as new in form, and it has taken on a new importance today.

SMARTSOURCING

Tom Koulopoulos, the incisive author of *Smartsourcing*, suggests that the process of globalization is far more than abundant and cheap labor. He sees the three trends of smartsourcing that motivate global outsourcing as cost, education, and mobility. Koulopoulos sees the process of wage arbitrage, through which lower wages for outsourcing can be used to reduce the costs of a service or product, as only the tip of the iceberg.

On education, he sees that higher education has created a new base of skilled, knowledgeable workers in countries with less developed economies. In 1950 in Japan, less than 1 percent of the population eligible for university actually attended; today in Japan that number is greater than 25 percent. The same sort of shift is occurring today in India and China, where college and university enrollment rates continue to multiply. This is already having a profound impact on the availability of qualified workers for jobs that U.S. companies would previously never have considered outsourcing. Work goes to the worker wherever they are.

On mobility, he sees that work can be moved with great ease today, to wherever it makes the most sense for the work to be done. Koulopoulos sees mobility of work as at least as great a factor in the modifying perspective of global trade as was the immigrant workers' flood into the United States in the 19th and early 20th centuries. Combining these three trends makes it clear that the depth and impact of outsourcing is far more than a fad.

Koulopoulos has found that many businesses that undertook an outsourcing initiative first did so as a cost benefit. The term he uses for this type of outsourcing is "lift and shift." This means an existing process is lifted out of its current organization and shifted to a third party.

The chosen third party may achieve what are called "economies of scope" through shared services, technology, or international wage arbitrage. This means that given the scope of more partners, there are better deals; a deeper knowledge of services allows for reduced cost opportunities and greater economic gains. However, such a relationship rarely leads to innovation on a higher level. Koulopoulos believes that this is one of the most limiting factors in the acceptance of outsourcing and off-shoring. Businesses need to focus their strategic resources on what they do best, and innovate using their core competencies. But they also need partners who can continue to innovate on noncore processes that they are outsourcing.

CORE COMPETENCY

Simply put, you cannot smartsource without a clear definition of your company's core competency, because you will not have the right base for partnering or collaborating on what isn't your core strength. Too many people define a core competency as either a product or service; they have a misplaced sense of what is essential.

Core competency runs much deeper in an organization's culture than a product or service. The understanding of your core competency is a key to accepting those factors or situations that detract from your resources. In a word, Koulopoulos argues that smartsourcing is about moving the business decision from an art form to a science. In manufacturing, those industries that delayed, or simply ignored, the move to off-shoring paid and will continue to pay a heavy price.

MANUFACTURING ROLES

Manufacturers have many roles to play. They can, and often do, excel as idea developers creating intellectual property. Some, such as IBM, excel, and have for a long time, as marketers. Some, such as Dell, are experts in developing a system of inbound suppliers. Others excel as assemblers, rather than manufacturers, of products. Some still make their one and only business manufacturing in a traditional sense, while others are finishers, packagers, and redevelopers of existing products.

The manufacturer is for all intents and purposes the origin of the supply chain—no goods, no supply chain. This is the reason that there are now so many different kinds of manufacturing. Manufacturing depends on getting the goods made, clearly, but also on getting the goods to the wholesaler, to the retailer, and sold. No one wants to manufacture simply to a warehouse; goods sitting are goods costing. This shift has forced change in manufacturing roles.

Today many more manufacturers are going virtual in the sense of actual production. They remain at the root of the product: planning, design, intellectual property ownership, information control, and selection of suppliers or a supplier/manufacturer. However, even some of these processes are "shipped" away. The major jobs of the manufacturer become branding, sales and marketing, control of the product's life cycle, spare part replacement, returns, and compliance with regulations.

Some manufacturers prefer to hold on to the task of final assembly, such as in the automotive and electronics industries. The supply lines for these kinds of manufacturing are most often extremely complex. In the case of automotive manufacturing, they can involve parts suppliers (e.g., Phillips head screws, washers, seals, gears) or suppliers making subassemblies (e.g., seats, airbags, tires, and transmissions). In some cases, the subassemblers are part of the manufacturing ownership, but in most cases today, it is pure outsourcing to another firm.

Manufacturers can become coordinators and designers of manufacturing, a role that fits Apple perfectly. Apple chooses its suppliers, puts demand on its suppliers, and controls, pays, and coordinates its suppliers. When we see a Bose stereo system built around an iPod, what exactly are we seeing? Is it iPod extended, or is it Bose taking advantage? Is it symbiotic or is it parasitic?

Sun Microsystems makes use of what it calls a "One Touch Supply Chain." This technique for its server business goes one step further than Apple. Sun has a third party manufacture and ship the product directly to the customer. Of course, the product is manufactured and shipped to Sun's specifications.

HEWLETT-PACKARD (HP)

HP is the 18th largest manufacturer in the world. HP innovates by breaking its manufacturing supply chain into business unit parts. It shares the Sun model by manufacturing its tape drives through full outsourcing. In other cases, it uses contract manufacturers or original design manufacturers.

Design for supply chain is a large part of Hewlett-Packard's supply chain strategy. It is used by product development teams and company engineers. The company saves in excess of $200 million a year using this process, which has six central goals:

1. The control of variety, as in the variety of components in products
2. Logistics enhancements that improve by design the density factor of a product and its size and its load on a pallet
3. The commonality and reuse of components in many models
4. Postponement of differentiation of components as in Europe and Asia—using therefore the same component (Different components can mean more design costs or more manufacturing costs, as there is variance in specifications.)
5. Tax and duty reduction by changing where the product is built and the cost of transferring the product
6. Take-back facilitation, as in reducing reverse supply costs—use, for instance, of socket connections rather than soldering (Some products are returned merely for the sake of a broken

solder connection. Use of sockets makes the connection less vulnerable and therefore less likely to be returned.)

HP claims that the use of these methods avoids the need (practiced by many) of pushing the problems of the supply chain on to the supplier. That is rampant in manufacturing and retailing, and it places inordinate squeeze problems on suppliers. It is easy for a manufacturer to look good if all problems are passed on to the supplier, including rock bottom costs. Suppliers feel squeezed when this is taken to an unfair level where they might lose money on their supply of parts or materials. They either play ball or lose the business. HP has to manage the risk of being supplied over 30 billion high-tech components a year—all are at risk in terms of price and availability. HP spends around $50 billion on supply chain activities. In many ways, HP can be considered a supply chain company.

IBM

IBM is the 14th largest manufacturer in the world. Its basic and applied research still hovers around computing technology, communication technology, and chip development. However, it presents itself as a solutions provider. In fact, IBM's core competency may be in its marketing, which is more technique, attitude, and presence than intellectual property. Is reliability a core competency? More than 50 percent of IBM's business is in service. Is its service knowledge its core competency? What happens to hardware? Is it possible to have two core competencies?

IBM sees itself as a deliverer of information systems. It also sees itself as a marketer of solutions to its clients, as with supply chain solutions. There is a two-tier system within IBM's supply chain business. The first tier is IBM's supply chain and its intricacies. The second tier is its supply chain service to its clients. This can be analyzed in six steps: (1) planning a supply chain strategy; (2) helping the client plan and manage the supply and demand across the whole supply chain;

(3) integrating the client's supply chain with a legacy ERP system or a new one; (4) helping the implementation of logistics throughout warehousing, transportation, and reverse processing (it seeks cost reduction, shortened development cycles, and increased quality of product and process); (5) assisting in the development of product lifecycle management that revolves around innovation and improved design; (6) and aiding in the improvement of the procurement process for greater efficiency, lower costs, tighter control of outlays, and improved service levels.

IBM started as a manufacturer of automated card readers, and then began manufacturing a string of mainframe products at multiple sites in the United States. It went through an extensive PC manufacturing phase, and now still manufacture servers and, of course, chips, among other products. It has evolved from a local manufacturer, to a national and now international manufacturer. Its business today is as much helping others manufacture as manufacturing themselves through its own manufacturing software and through extensive consulting services. IBM has grown with the times. It has breadth in its business; it goes from chips to consultants, from products to solutions for its clients.

IBM PROCESS ENHANCING

In a big action, IBM has moved its whole procurement management to Shenzhen, China. It is a bold move and follows on a long-term position of doing business in China. IBM spends $40 billion a year on external suppliers, and by moving to China, it is getting closer to a vast majority of those suppliers. Service is 51 percent of IBM's business, but that leaves 49 percent for electronic hardware—and at IBM's scale, that is a great deal. Part of its move to Shenzhen is to help develop local talent and this means executives as well. IBM already has 1,850 employees in the area.

DELL

Dell was founded in 1984, and was offering next-day, on-site product services by 1987. By 1996, customers were buying computers through the Internet. Dell also extended its business from notebook and desktop computers to servers in 1996. It opened for business in Xiamen, China, in 1998. By the year 2000, Dell's sales were about $50 million a day.

By way of innovating, it built—and still builds—one-off computers to the specifications of customers. Its supply chain and distribution system is geared for an assembly of one product at a time. Dell has a staggering 20,000 suppliers and no warehouses. Its supply is direct from supplier to its assembly points and to the minute. This vast number of suppliers includes manufacturers of components in Taiwan, China, and Malaysia. It makes use of U.S.-based shipping partners (3PLs), allowing Dell faster reaction to customer demand than its competition.

During the union shut down of 29 West Coast ports, Dell's logistics team chartered eighteen 747s (a 747 configured for cargo can hold the equivalent of 10 tractor-trailers) from UPS, Northwest Airlines, and China Airlines at $500,000 per plane. Each plane could carry parts for 10,000 PCs, and the company's needs, usually handled by sea, were filled by air instead. That is the supply chain in action.

PROCESS ENHANCING

Dell's control of suppliers is all worked around timing along with high quality expectations. It operates within an ultralean set of logistics and manufacturing processes. It builds 80,000 computers each day, with only two hours of inventory in each factory. That has to be an apex in lean manufacturing. Lean manufacturing is minimal manufacturing in the sense of least cost, highest value, greatest quality, and maximally efficient supply and distribution. It is sometimes also referred to as agile manufacturing. New orders come into the factory at the rate of one every 20 seconds over the Internet. Dell's suppliers have 90 minutes to truck their parts to the assembly line. The Dell model drives inventory often into supplier warehouses despite all efforts to avoid inventory. For example, MMC Technology supplies disks for hard drives and it holds inventory in order to fill the huge orders from Dell.

Dell has taken away the golden parachute of ample inventory. Dell's suppliers are tightly integrated into the flow of its supply chain. Demand management is what Dell is all about; in some respects it is the symbol and the epitome of on-demand consumer fulfillment. It may not have invented the idea of a manufacture of one and a customer of one, but in the eyes of business, analysts, and, to some extent, the public, Dell is the on-demand solution for one customer.

DELL'S CORE COMPETENCY

Is Dell's core competency actually the supply chain process? Is core competency the ability of this company to organize itself successfully so that it can carry out such a strategy day by day? It buys to plan and builds to order, and all of this depends on its knowing exactly where everything is in the process cycle. The prerequisite is a high level of visibility of the demand process by the second. Dell has mastered the ability to move from manufacturing one type of legacy computer system to ramping up fast for a new model. This clearly is demonstrated by the fact that it had 22 product families in 1998, and was able to increase this to 175 by 2005.

SUMMING UP: MANUFACTURING

We have seen how today's manufacturing no longer requires spaces such as plants and factories. We have seen that there are many different roles that can be called manufacturing, including not really manufacturing at all outside of controlling a virtual process. We have seen how three companies, Hewlett-Packard, IBM, and Dell, have fit into these new models of manufacturing with their emphasis on supply chain management, tight agile manufacturing, and split-second supply. We have seen that an on-demand, "make it for one customer" model is giving strategic advantage to a company such as Dell. Manufacturing today has fully embraced the pull model of business, bringing about global sourcing, new methods of outsourcing, and a premium on partnering.

Chapter 12

SILKS TO CELLS: RETAIL EVOLUTION

Retailing may have started with a combination of abundance and willingness to collaborate or trade—too much of one thing in one place and not of another in another place. Balance is what retailing is all about.

We do not really know when bartering and bargaining was born, but Southern Arabia (now Syria, Iraq, and Iran) is a good bet. Grain silos in some early villages indicate a surplus of grains. They farmed outside the town and lived or stored inside. The first towns needed to draw on the food supplies from the surrounding area. This meant supply lines by roads (paths) or rivers or seas.

In ancient Sumer, the earliest city stores were bazaars, open markets in plazas or open areas. These would have been near rivers, lakes, and ocean shores. Storage of grain, water, and metals (ores) must have made one city dominant over others in whatever category they were favored. The region, or the city-state, or the proto-nation was the organizing force behind the development.

Storage is the key to trading. If a society uses all it makes, it has nothing to trade. If it buys more than it makes, it has a problem. Storage and trading spread to Europe with bazaars, markets, and plazas, and, in time, to great trading companies such as the historic Dutch East India Company.

CHAIN STORES

Retailing went beyond the trading store as cities really developed and came into their own as centers of population. Retailing as we know it today was a gathering of goods by type: clothing, notions, food, alcohol, weapons, horse goods, or hats. New cities, private enterprise, and urban infrastructure called for stores such as Marshall Field's, R.H. Macy, Gimbels, Bests, and Woolworth.

The late 1920s and early 1930s saw the beginning of national products such as Wonder Bread and Hostess. National sales, national marketing, and national advertising were born in those years, spread by outdoor signs and newspaper and magazine ads. National advertising was an outgrowth of New York ad agencies extending their power, and was a means by which to counteract the declining sales brought about by the Depression.

By 1929, there were already supermarket chains and the beginning of the march toward "big box" warehouse stores. Innovation by managers and business entrepreneurs brought about the first shopping center in Valley Plaza, California, in 1951, followed by a massive number nationally in a decade. The first shopping mall appeared in Dallas in the 1930s, while the 1940s saw the first 7-Eleven convenience store in Texas along with the advent of broadcast TV and the accompanying store advertisements.

CREDIT CARDS

When Franklin National Bank in New York issued the first credit cards in 1951, another tool was added to retailing. In 1962, Sam Walton opened his first Wal-Mart, which was soon followed by Kmart and

Target Stores. In 1967, Kroger installed its first bar code scanner in a Cincinnati supermarket. Therefore, bar coding as we recognize it is 40 years old. Wal-Mart integrated its distribution system and became a practitioner of J-I-T in 1969, as did wise motor companies in Japan.

That same year, DHL started, and two years later, FedEx was founded and a new form of express service was born. Retail mergers and acquisitions occurred in large numbers. The 1982 coining of the word *Internet* probably went unnoticed for a few years.

The march of the big stores went on. In 1990, the Mall of America opened just outside of Minneapolis. It was and still is the largest mall in the United States, with 2.5 million square feet of store space, 12,500 parking places, and 520 stores. In 1993, Sears dropped its merchandise catalog, an important signal that retailing had changed dramatically. CompUSA opened in 1994 and became one of a few computer-centered stores to survive the late 1990s. In 1995, Amazon.com sold its first book online, and by 1996, the Internet was taking the world into a new information age with eBay auctions, spam, polls, still pictures, videos, and much more.

NATIONAL OR INTERNATIONAL?

Most multinational stores try to do two things: succeed and fit in without losing brand identity. It is an interesting act and does not always work, as Wal-Mart learned with its stores in Germany. A different set of consumers can mean different buying needs, expectations, and ambience. For instance, Germans are not accustomed to having their goods placed in bags, as is standard at Wal-Mart. This and other customer misjudgments and labor mishandling brought about their failure in Germany.

Demand management is about the adaptive response to customers as needs change and as the availability of new technology makes the functions of what those needs are change. It is about the share of a customer, the degree to which they come back for more of the same or more of related products and services. This is a newer measure of the customer. A share is a different way to look at a customer. The traditional market view is to count the number of customers, and not the degree of buy-in by a single customer. So if you focus in on the one customer, you want to get his or her attention to pricier items, and more of those like their first choice.

CUSTOMERS/CONSUMERS

Customer needs have to be measured against the availability of the supplies necessary to fulfill that need. This activity is global in nature, and changes in hours or seconds. It is about following the changing needs of the customer. The only way these changes can be followed is by a combination of tracking and feedback. Changes in customer need affect design, manufacturing, commerce, and marketing. A synchronized supply chain goes further and allows for the means of anticipating customer need. This is a benefit of the speed of the process combined with its visibility and its insight into the posture of the customer.

The consumer (a customer who buys) is the core engine within supply chain demand. Consumers are fickle, there are always more of them each day, and they only want what they want when they want it. They expect ample and quality products. If they are disappointed, they don't hesitate to go elsewhere. Consumers are the most complex part of the supply chain.

STRETCHING

Retailing now has to face what might be called the double stretch. It has to accomplish fulfillment of goods at a faster and faster pace to keep up with consumer demand and the variability of season, place, new product introductions, and competition. But retailers also face longer and longer supply chains and more and more suppliers.

Retailing is the engine that creates the demand for products, new products, and newer-than-new products. Without demand, the supply chain is an abstraction and manufacturing becomes an exercise in futility. If people at dealerships don't want your car, then your car is redundant. If the only people who want your car are the managers and workers who make the product, then you are in big trouble.

Wal-Mart supplies itself with one shipping container per minute to stock its stores. IKEA is smart; it lets customers deliver the goods themselves. Their compact products make this possible. A store today is an experience, and is thus more than an outlet for the sale and distribution of goods.

RETAILING AND CORE COMPETENCIES

It is important, of course, for a company to put its core competency first and foremost. One assumes that in most cases, core competency means developing and guarding of intellectual property. Is intellectual property the same as core competency? Well, some very successful companies appear to operate without any real intellectual property at all.

What, for instance, is Wal-Mart's intellectual property? Its core competency is simply its operational ability to beat the competition. It does this by cutting everything superfluous, and concentrating on getting the right product to the right customer at the right time at the right price.

APPLE STORE

Apple is not really in the retailing business, but its stores act as machines that sell machines. Everything is out where the customer can get at it, play with it, and watch others play with it; everything is set up for full consumer participation. There is no visible selling. The customers sell themselves. The checkout is massive and busy.

Apple sees customer reaction in depth. Its store in New York sells not only its own products but products related to its products that are produced by other manufacturers, such as Bose sound systems.

The Apple Store is a test for product interest on the part of the customer and for customer feedback that can affect design, function, and volume of a product. This in turn feeds into the supply chain as modifications of manufacturing volumes, parts volumes, and the scale of transport and distribution. The store acts as a remote sensor for the supply chain.

SUMMING UP: RETAIL EVOLUTION

Retail began with a society's surplus and the opportunity to trade. It quickly coalesced into bazaars and then stores, marts, and big box retailers with the advent of cities and ever more advanced forms of transportation to get goods from one place to another. The specialization of retailing, as with food and clothing, evolved into once again a gathering into marts and malls. If you want to open a new store that is built on a new model, it might be better to look at theatres or museums or sports arenas to get an idea. You need an idea and not a building.

Chapter 13

THE STORE'S THE THING: RETAILING AND THE SUPPLY CHAIN

Making the retail supply chain easy can be difficult. Retailers need every advantage they can find to differentiate themselves from each other. This includes tuning up the supply chain, increasing margins, making positive steps in innovation, and working intelligently with diverse sources.

RETAIL SUPPLY BUYING TODAY

Sue Welch, CEO of Boston-based TradeStone Software, is a seasoned veteran of the global supply chain business. Her company offers retailers a "unified buying process." This process can be applied to sourcing a vendor across the street or on the other side of the world. Welch says that the typical buying process is bifurcated geographically. To buy goods from one geographic region, one needs to use a specific process, while dealing with particular partners requires another process. TradeStone learns their clients' purchasing needs, and then unifies those processes to encompass all geographic regions, partners, and technologies so that it becomes transparent to the user.

Just as we must ask the final customers what they want and then set up a means by which to get it to them, so someone must ask the stores what they want to buy for these customers. It is a cycle. The process of buying has to be easy and intuitive. The key to getting technology used and used properly is to make it easy to adopt and implement. It must help them to think naturally. It has to be intuitive. How do the product developers think? How do people who are sourcing think? How does the entire supply chain "think"? Buyers' and sellers' means of thinking can be organized into coherent steps, which can then be documented and built into a procedural system. Then, according to Welch, they don't need to worry about foreign currencies or about language.

We need to ask if a solution like TradeStone's system can mean increased margins. Welch suggests that people don't really understand how much they are paying for goods. Their margins are worn down from two forces: unexpected expenses and the inability to sell their goods. Showing them the real expenses will allow them to price the goods correctly in order to increase their margins. This results in having a technology that supports responses to rapidly changing conditions. Instead of taking months to respond to something because of tracking from different systems, the information is now presented instantly. Businesses are then able to respond to rapid price changes and become more innovative in what they present.

Welch's solution bridges the gap between forecasting and execution. TradeStone creates a plan, puts that out to bid and to be sourced, and determines where their clients are with regard to plan and margin. It compares what has been manufactured relative to the plan. Then TradeStone goes through the supply chain (shipping, logistics, and payment process) and compares the plan to the actual progress, making adjustments to the plan as necessary.

OUTSOURCING BY RETAILERS

The outsourcing (buying overseas specifically) by retailers has changed the face of world trade. It brings on imbalances in money, pressure on overseas suppliers, and many problems of ground, water, and air pollution that I will spare you. What is important to understand is the huge growth of shipping containers. The number of containers being shipped into the United States grew from 1.11 million containers in 2002 to 2.49 million just three years later. The majority of these materials and products are from Asia, predominantly China.

However, growth in the other direction—exporting—is negligible, growing from 641,200 containers in 2002 to only 973,600 in the year 2005.

RETAILERS' SUPPLY NETWORKS

The nature of retailing has changed as the supply chain has changed. There are more suppliers, more products, more distant suppliers, more competition for suppliers, and more complex demand from consumers. Retail is growing and groaning worldwide.

TRUCKING DEPENDENT

A truck is the standard means of supply for nearly all stores. The supply of merchandise to the store is the most vital single link in a supply chain. It is not merely a question of getting the goods there. That is important, but more important is getting the goods there *on time.* These goods need to be the right goods (diet cola, not regular), they must be undamaged as far as possible (no broken eggs), and unspoiled (no rotten vegetables). What is more, the information attached to the goods, bills of lading, and scans from bar codes have to match what was ordered. All this is a tall order for 3PLs and store-owned fleets that do the picking up, driving, and delivering. There are a thousand opportunities to spoil a good delivery. The warehouse and the distribution center are key tools along with the truck driver and the fleet managers.

WAL-MART

Sam Walton opened his first Wal-Mart in Bentonville, Arkansas, in 1962. The principal idea for which the store has been tagged is low cost and massive inventory and variety of goods. Among the company's first moves was the purchase of other stores, which were then converted to Wal-Mart stores. This move was accompanied by going national. By 1970, it opened the first Wal-Mart distribution center in Bentonville in an early move toward supply chain mastery.

Wal-Mart now excels in distribution centers (DCs). Its DC in Hopkinsville, Kentucky, is 1.2 million square feet. A typical Wal-Mart DC is 10 times the size of its average store. Its DCs have 250 docking stations and can serve typically 500 big rigs a day. Needless to say, they are busy places and in some way, they represent the edge Wal-Mart has in its marketplace: Wal-Mart has 61,000 suppliers, 85 percent of American households shop at Wal-Mart, Wal-Mart is growing at about 14 percent a year, and it is expected to be the first company to reach $1 trillion in sales.

Let me say that for Wal-Mart it isn't just more stores or bigger stores. It isn't just new ways to discount and lower prices. It is essentially about the enhancing of process in retailing. Wal-Mart is strong because it thinks ahead and organizes its suppliers as a whole. It isn't just bar codes and RFID—although its use and mandating of the latter has placed Wal-Mart ahead.

Wal-Mart has a certain amount of store type (mostly dry goods or food) and scale differential (30,000 to 224,000 square feet). Its discount stores average about 100,000 square feet, while its Super Centers are larger, at 187,000 square feet on average. It also owns Sam's Club, a discount shopping club in the form of a warehouse. Sam's Club specializes in groceries and consumables in large quantities.

These stores are competitive with Costco. Sam's Club is interesting in that it takes Wal-Mart's dominance of warehousing technique one step closer to the customer. Its warehouses or distribution centers can handle up to 220 tractor-trailer deliveries a day. It has figured out by looking at its customers what the customers are likely to want to carry home in their big SUVs. Lots of paper products, water in many forms and by the case, canned food, and bulk boxes of cereal, to name but a few. Sam's Club is in this way like IKEA who figured people would carry their furniture home if it were packed for easy loading and carrying. These small acts of genius make a store king of hill.

WAL-MART ASSOCIATES

More than 1.3 million associates work for Wal-Mart in the United States—more than the populations of 12 states. The company has another 500,000 associates overseas. Wal-Mart operates stores in 44 countries, with its first store abroad opening in Mexico City in 1991. It now has 2,276 stores abroad. It has more than 100,000 employees in Mexico alone, and does $56.3 billion in sales overseas. It increased its international business in 2005 by 18.3 percent over 2004, and increased its international operating profits to nearly $3 billion. However, its troubles in international markets may put a damper on the continuation of that kind of company growth, as will be discussed later in this chapter.

RFID AND WAL-MART

When you process one container a minute you had better have a means of tracking. Wal-Mart's mandate has been that by the end of 2006, it will have about one third of its stores "wired" for RFID. As the United States' and the world's largest retailer, this means that those doing business with Wal-Mart and its RFID mandate will have to comply or give up the business. Wal-Mart is tagging at the pallet level and at the case level, but not yet at the item level yet. The pallets contain the cases, and the cases contain the individual and packaged products.

Wal-Mart's distribution centers, where all this happens, are located strategically as close to its stores and good infrastructure as possible. The distribution center is the core of Wal-Mart's supply chain strategy. Wal-Mart has set the standard here with DC teams that have become the company's lifeblood and its advantage in the marketplace. Orders and order fulfillment are as good as the synchronous teams that handle them. Inventory, which can cost money as it sits, can be dealt with as goods in process, and this translates into value added and profit.

GOING GLOBAL

The multistore acquisition of ASDA in the U.K., and of Seiyu in Japan, have become the model for how Wal-Mart's rollouts in new countries will be accomplished. Go into a country, pick a sizeable retailer, buy the entire chain, and then change the name. Voilá: a multitude of Wal-Mart stores with discounting in place, new technology behind it, and an awesome scale of retailing and supply chain systems.

The reality is in the prices but the prices are merely a reflection of their supply chains. Some analysts expect Wal-Mart to grow at 14 percent a year over the next five years, a higher rate of growth than the economy of China. Wal-Mart will do it by growing electronic sales as with iPods, printers, and laptops. It will grow by pushing its supermarket arena products. It will grow as it sets up stores in nation after nation.

WAL-MART OVERSEAS

Wal-Mart operates retail stores in, among other places, Mexico (774 stores), Puerto Rico (54), Canada (263), Argentina (11), Brazil (295), and China (56). The company has sold its stores in Germany and South Korea. (All figures are from 2005.)

Not all is perfect for Wal-Mart. It failed to gain a foothold in Germany. There are many reasons why. The biggest is that in Germany a retailer cannot sell at below manufacturer's suggested retail price. Wal-Mart's strength is in its ability to sell items more cheaply than the competition, so if it can't do this, what else does it have to offer? They don't really offer ambience, special customer handling, or great follow-up for the customer.

During 2005, Wal-Mart started its move into India. As of 2006, it is not only building stores in other countries, it is building its own distribution centers that are the logistics hubs where they receive and sort goods to stock the stores in the area. Therefore, the commitment within these countries is more than providing stores. It is a full supply chain system and all the logistics that can go into it. For instance, China's 56 stores are serviced by several distribution centers. These centers, like their stores, have local associates (in China) and they number in the tens of thousands. Wal-Mart is exporting a retailing and supply chain system that not only trains and influences its employees but the public as well.

WAL-MART CUSTOMERS

People in these many countries become Wal-Mart customers. They will live with the results of Wal-Mart's commitment to radio frequency identification (RFID). The power of Wal-Mart is partly derived from its partnerships and its bold use of technology. These two things in combination give Wal-Mart the muscle to knock out much of the competition, for better or worse, regardless of state or nation. Retail Forward, Inc. has predicted that Wal-Mart will top $500 billion in sales by 2010. That will translate into more power and more countries and retailing dominance.

The trade of the world, as we have said, moves in shipping containers. In 2005, 17.3 million containers were imported into the United States. Of that, 1 out of 25 was destined for the retail giant Wal-Mart. Those containers were earmarked for a recognized demand.

IKEA

IKEA was not the first knock-down furniture store or manufacturer. Way back in 1730, the Frenchman Jacob Schuebler invented a collapsible bed. It could be taken apart and set up in minutes and would pack flat. Camp furniture first used by the military predated even Schuebler. However, it took IKEA to make it one of the keystones of a very successful business. It is a store that has become for many a way of life.

The founder, Ingvar Kamprad, registered the company in Sweden in 1943 and opened its first store in Almhult, Sweden, in 1958. The company expanded first to Norway, then to Switzerland, and then, in 1985, to the United States. It moved to international stores and serving international customers early on, and its move to the United States was made despite the impression that the United States already had everything. Two thousand suppliers around the world supply the company with manufactured furniture and other products, as it does not manufacture anything itself.

It controls the quality tightly and provides the design. Its teams work within the suppliers' factories, keeping tabs on original materials such as raw wood, from its sawmilling, processing, use in furniture, packing, storage, and eventual transport. The quality control of the supplier and of IKEA therefore becomes one and the same.

ONE MILLION A DAY

Three hundred sixty-five million people visited IKEA stores in 2004. Many had, before they arrived, perused one of the tens of millions of catalogs (only the Bible beats IKEA in volumes published worldwide) to determine what they might buy. They came to see and sit on, or measure, or consider the furniture while they took the long and winding tour of this enormous store. An IKEA store covers over 350,000 square feet, more than twice the size of a normal Wal-Mart store facility.

The company's growth has also been big. It skyrocketed from 3.8 billion euros in 1994 to 12.6 billion euros ($15.5 billion in U.S. dollars) in 2004. The company's more than 215 stores carry up to 12,000 products. The basic wooden furniture is made in Eastern Europe, which means a good deal of shipping is involved. IKEA has become a master of the supply chain.

STEVE & BARRY'S

Steve & Barry's is a chain that features a broad line of apparel with a focus on sportswear and related accessories. Its stores grew out of a single university community and into over 130 stores in 33 states. It has grown by 100 percent over the past few years. It is rumored that on some items, Steve & Barry's beats Wal-Mart on price. Its stores tend to be 50,000 square feet and larger, and that size makes them attractive to malls. Gary Sugarman, the company's COO, came out of the financial world rather than the retail world. One of his inventions is a think tank–like group of people at the company that analyze new ideas and business models. This is RAND—the famous analytical think tank that tries to create manageable solutions to large problems, thinking at a store level.

RAND also focus on warehouse logistics, merchandise-pricing strategy, and store management that may concentrate on recruitment and training of personnel. Steve & Barry's has licensing agreements with companies such as Coors Brewing Company, General Mills, Hershey's, and Yamaha for logos used on their jackets, jeans, and broad line of apparel and accessories. One of its prime strategies is to buy directly from foreign sources, but cut its costs by accepting longer lead times. This gives its suppliers a more steady production throughout the year.

Steve & Barry's auto-replenishment system distributes goods based on daily sales analysis, seasonal fit, and inventory. The systems allow it to replenish a need within three days of the initial detected trend of a store's depletion.

TRACKING

Steve & Barry's system tracks through sales, alerts its distribution center (DC) to pull merchandise, sends trucks from the DC to the stores, and then unloads merchandise and places it on the sales floor. Its centralized DC in Ohio is a very large 1.5 million square feet and serves all of its stores.

Steve & Barry's cleverly uses direct truck floor loading instead of palettes to maximize the use of space for products in each truckload. The company currently sources from over 30 different countries, of which one-third are in Africa, one-third in Asia, and one-third in the Americas. The typical product life cycle (going from creation to fully stocked items in the store) ranges from several months (long lead times allow the company to keep prices low), to a few weeks for items such as T-shirts. Long leads are a clever way of maintaining the connection to suppliers.

The company is currently working to make everything in its distribution center automated. Clearly every retailer aims for 100 percent in-stock positioning, but Steve & Barry's keeps its replenishment within a 90 percent to 95 percent range. In its DC, it has over 40,000 SKUs (store keeping units—unique combinations of style, design, and color).

However, there are exceptions to the automated stock system. In special cases, the corporate planning team overrides the automated system and is able to track the sales that have been coming in and predict which stores will need more merchandise urgently. This can mean stepping in to get merchandise to those stores in advance of depletion, or using faster shipping methods. Steve & Barry's is a good example of high-gear adaptive behavior. It appears to operate in real time, or as close to it as possible. It is customer-centric through its scale of available goods and in association with price. It is moving toward item-level digital control.

SUMMING UP: RETAIL AND THE SUPPLY CHAIN

Today's successful retail stores have several things in common. They focus on the customer. They operate highly tuned supply chains and they innovate on the run. They may discount, but they get those goods the customer wants in sufficient quantity to be able to fulfill the endless needs of even one customer. They are getting a handle on their supply chains through more sensitive tracking methodologies such as RFID, and this means even greater control over stock and the right flow of materials to fit with the flow of the information tracking the materials. If you want to start a store, begin with the customer's needs and work backward from there. Figure out a way to deliver goods better, cheaper, and within an ambience that makes people return again and again.

Chapter 14

PORTS, SHIPS, HUBS, AND RAILS: INTERMODAL TRANSPORTATION

At numerous points in the supply chain, goods (container and bulk) move from one mode of transportation to another. They go from one port to another, from one carrier to another, and from a single-handed implementation to a collaborative one. Let's talk about different ports first and then hubs; about intermodal transport, collaboration, and rails; and finally and briefly about trucking.

The supply chain and its logistics require places of origin and places of reception. Each place of reception has particular characteristics. Ports have tools for loading and unloading, warehouses to store, and facilities for offices, customs, and other functions. If they are container ports, they also have a massive number of containers. If they are bulk ports, they have different cranes, different storage facilities, and different ships visiting them. Canals act as the means of passage between two bodies of water, such as the Atlantic and the Pacific, and help serve the ports. Most canals have port facilities, a series of elaborate locks, and the means to energize their movement, as well as offices and a terminal building for customs, storage, and goods seizure.

Airports have a whole different set of tools and terminals. Airports are most often near a large city. When they act as cargo hubs, they may be selected to give ground support infrastructure. Airports have hangars, warehouses, or distribution centers and act as intermodal facilities, connecting planes to trucks and, in some cases, to rail. Each of these modes has its transport means: containerships, railroad cars, tractor trailers, and cargo planes.

PORTS AS THE NEW BATTLEFIELD

The carriers of most of the world's goods are either tankers or containerships. The economy of their use by the shipping companies has called for larger and larger ships. Big is not always better, however. Many of the newest ships are already too big to go through the Panama Canal. Some large tankers are too big to go through the Suez Canal.

Locks control the connection between two bodies of water such as a lake and river, or an ocean and a sea. The differential between water levels determines the scale and number of locks required to lift or lower ships, barges, and boats. Locks and ships are a match, or should be, but today they are not. Ships can be built faster than locks, and many of today's ships are too large for the existing locks.

Today's Panamax locks are restricted to vessels that are less than 106 feet wide and 965 feet long. As new locks are built, they will accommodate larger ships, up to 180 feet wide and 1,265 feet long. These restrictions define the limits of what can go where in the world. Suez Canal specifications can accommodate ships with drafts up to 64 feet wide and of any length.

The ports themselves are in a furious contest to outperform their competition. Shanghai, already the third largest port in the world, has recently opened Yanghan Deep Water Port on an island. It is slated to become the largest port ever and will, in time, handle in excess of 20 million containers a year. The port expects to spend $1.2

billion a year. In comparison, the United States spends only about $2 billion on *all* of its ports each year.

U.S. ports are in constant use, moving 95 percent of the United States' overseas trade by weight and 75 percent of its trade by value. Overseas trade has been increasing at about twice the measure of the GNP. This means that these ports are in a sense the nation's aorta—and it is in serious danger of being blocked.

The six leading container ports are all in Asia and there seems to be little to suggest that the trend toward Asian dominance in port size and capacity, and containers handled and shipped, will diminish. The Asian ports are in better shape than U.S. or European ports on a port facilities basis, but they hold a less advantageous position in regard to supporting infrastructure. Road and rail systems in China need enormous upgrade, as they do to an even greater degree in India where roads, rails, and ports suffer.

The growth of ports in the last six years has averaged 10 percent. The five largest container ports are Hong Kong; Singapore; Shanghai; Shenzhen, China; and Busan, South Korea—all Asian. Security efforts should start at these ports, and not on the arrival at the destination ports of ships out of these ports.

The incursion of the security issue has many ramifications for these ports and their operating companies. The United States appears to be leading the field in technology for security. However, no port anywhere has full security. The scaling up of ships in TEU carrying capacity will exacerbate all of these issues. There will be enormous need for more trucking and intermodal rail technology. The sheer length and capacity of a 15,000 TEU ship will call for more cranes, more space, more access, and more security by well-trained and responsible people.

PORT OPERATORS

The large port operators are in most cases not of the nationality of the port. The sea world is used to this disjunction, as most ships bearing

U.S. goods, for instance, fly a foreign flag. Large operators handle an enormous number of containers. PSA International processes 42.18 million containers a year at 19 ports worldwide, including the massive port of Singapore. Dubai Ports World handles 33 million containers yearly, or about 9 percent of the world's container business and growing.

Both Dubai Ports World and PSA are partially dwarfed by the king of port operators: Hutchinson Port Holdings handles 47.8 million containers at the ports it operates. There appears to be no fear, despite continued mergers, of a dwindling base of world port operators. The top 10 operators currently control about 50 percent of the container shipping business, and there are many other contenders, including some quite large shipping carriers.

The world's deep sea ports are the trading center giants of today's supply network. Global trade depends on deep ports, as they are the only ports that can take all sizes of containerships, supertankers, and bulk load ships. The GDP of a nation is geared to these ports and their condition, and, as in China, they act as a guarantee for future growth at about 10 percent yearly.

BIG SHIPS

The newest containerships can be over 300 meters in length (about the size of our largest aircraft carriers) and require a deeper draft than most ports have available. It would be a disaster to get over 100,000 tons of cargo stuck on a sandbar. The recently built Lxel Maersk containership is 352-plus meters (1,385 feet) in length; it needs room to navigate, and that means port depth.

It is little wonder that the powerhouse of shipping carriers, Maersk Line, is now laying the keel for a 15,000 TEU containership. This nearly doubles the existing capacity of the largest containerships, and will place a great burden on those ports unable to deal with either the multiple crane capacity or the infrastructure of intermodal trucking services that support transportation.

How big is too big with these ships?

SHIPPING CONTAINERS

The world's most common means of mass goods transport is the shipping container. There are in excess of 200 million container trips per year worldwide and these trips require 18 million containers to fill the bill. Because the container business is increasing at a rate of about 10 percent a year, this means an increasing number of containership loads moving simultaneously.

Since September 11, one of the nation's most persistent vulnerabilities has been the 17,000 shipping containers that enter the United States from around the world every day. Now a host of companies are looking to see what they can do to solve the problem.

Container inspection of 17,000 containers a day is the U.S. shipping industry's challenge. Now that the U.S. government has mandated inspection, the idea will be to inspect every container. Today, only about 2 percent of containers are inspected by customs officials, according to the Brookings Institution. If the United States were to inspect all six to seven million containers a year, the cost would skyrocket. In cases that require detailed human intervention, a single inspection can be a high as $5,000. This could mean up to $35 billion a year to fully inspect all the containers, and the number of containers is only increasing.

According to Drewry Shipping Consultants, as the industry moves forward, some of the most significant business action will be in the carrier-stevedore partnership arrangements. Drewry secs involvement of the two large shippers, Mediterranean Shipping and COSCO, in this activity. It also predicts the business of carriers, containers, and ports being driven by Asian development, and particularly by China. It expects that about 40 percent of total world trade will be Far East–generated by 2009. Drewry further suggests that the surge in trade will witness the outstripping of supply by demand. It is inevitable given the continued pressure of population, the move of nonindustrial nations to industrial nations, and the move by business to improve and enlarge.

AIR HUBS

Air hubs are airports that have been designed with crew changes in mind. They are most particularly suited for UPS, DHL, and FedEx because these companies don't have to worry about passengers inbound or outbound.

The largest air cargo hub in the world is in Memphis, which handled 3,554,575 metric tons of cargo in 2004. The next four largest are Hong Kong, Tokyo (Narita), Anchorage, and Seoul. Of the five leaders, three are in Asia, and much of Anchorage's cargo is Asian trade into the United States. Memphis is at the top simply because it is the central hub of FedEx—and FedEx has centered its future on the China trade.

Memphis is in the number one position for cargo, is centrally located in the United States, and has a road system that radiates north, south, east, and west, making it an ideal location for the major hub of FedEx.

The Hong Kong airport can take advantage of the huge and growing China trade and its modern airport facility. It is number one in international cargo throughput. Its new Super Terminal is the world's largest at 330,000 square meters. The terminal features an automated cargo handling system. Hong Kong is a DHL hub.

Tokyo Narita is Japan's busiest airport with leading-edge export and import facilities. It is the major hub for All Nippon Airways (ANA) and also serves FedEx. It does business with 52 airlines and 35 countries, and has good rail access.

Anchorage, Alaska, is a major hub that serves Asian-to-U.S. business and is a critical link for FedEx, UPS, and USPS. FedEx out of Anchorage can handle 13,400 packages per hour, while UPS handles around 5,000. USPS has a large sectional facility there for all ZIP codes in Alaska. The airport is growing, but already is the fourth largest cargo port in the world.

Seoul Incheon Airport, located outside of Seoul on Yeongjong Island, is South Korea's largest and busiest airport. It is the hub of both Korea Air and Asiana Airlines. It also serves UPS and FedEx.

The major carriers have a big effect on airports, or, in a way, the airports are the facilities that make their business possible.

Louisville is the main air hub for UPS (other UPS hubs also rank high, such as Dallas, which is number 25 in the world). The most distinguishing factor, both economically and by scale, is the increased use of the airport by UPS for its heavy airfreight. It is the presence of UPS's World Port distribution center that highlights Louisville.

Los Angeles International has the geographical positioning of Los Angeles as an important reason for its position in cargo handling. Los Angeles is the biggest U.S. container port. This leads to great opportunity for intermodal freight traffic. It has a huge, though overwhelmed, road system for freight delivery.

Miami International is the major U.S. Latin American air cargo link. It has recently added LAN Cargo to its facilities, and LAN is the number two freight carrier in Miami behind UPS. FedEx and DHL, and a great number of smaller carriers and freight companies, also serve the airport.

INTERMODAL AND RAIL

Intermodal transportation goes in the teeth of accepted practice. Accepted practice reinforces union rules, proprietary business goals, governmental structure, and the ever-present strength of human apathy: not invented here, not our thing, it's the other guys. Rail created the problem in the 19th century. The advent of trucking was not thought at first as a serious threat. In time, the nature of, and the capacity of trucking, made it a first-rate competitor to rail. The same things happened in regard to valuable cargo with the incursions of airfreight. Air does not deliver bulk goods or traditional containers to any real extent, but air is fast, and valued goods can be valued for money or by the level of need, or both. The problem now is how to create transfers of goods at rail yards and terminals, air hubs, sea ports and terminals, and trucking facilities and distribution centers.

Each mode has a medium with which, or along which, it moves: planes by air, trucks by roads, rail by tracks. Between each of these are yards, hubs, gateways, airports, stations, warehouses, distribution centers, and garages. According to Jim Martin, an intermodal expert, the concept of intermodal or multimodal transportation starts back in 1954, when a favorable ICC ruling made it possible for railroads to handle trailers and containers on flatcars. This ruling led to "piggyback" service, the loading of more than one container on top of another aboard a rail car.

RAIL TO TRUCK AND TRUCK TO RAIL

The most frequent intermodal exchange is between trucks and trucks. The next most is between rail and trucks and rail and rail. We have had more experience with these forms of transfer, but that does not mean that it works well today. In addition, trucks are the normal means by which airfreight is moved out of or into an airport.

All of the following modes have their place: sea to truck, sea to rail, truck to truck, truck to rail, truck to air, and back again. The choice should not be based on lazy convenience but on savings in fuel, reduction in transportation costs, savings in labor, reduction of accidents, increased safety, and better pollution standards. The choice should be made with efficiency and J-I-T in mind. The choice is simple: Either a shipping enterprise collaborates today, or it may flounder tomorrow. Intermodal application can be expedited by fleet management in the case of trucking and particularly by collaboration through the services of 3PLs. No enterprise (shipper, retailer, and manufacturer) is so big or small that it should avoid collaborating intelligently in the ever-expanding $3 trillion global logistics market (a figure calculated by the Omni Consulting Group).

Gil Carmichael, the senior chair of the Intermodal Transportation Institute and former Federal Railroad Administrator, suggests that intermodal transportation is the core element of an intelligent logistics infrastructure. He believes this because it is the system that really delivers the goods. It does so in a way that enhances equipment and the use of people (and can add to the economics). It builds on the inherent strengths of each of the participating transportation modes, maximizing benefits such as fuel efficiency, reduced environmental impact, and safety. It measures delivery by means of it being expeditious; that means that the intermodal system provides the customer greater flexibility in choices of the modes of transportation such as trucks or rail, the routes they take (in both cases very different), and levels of service (to the door, overnight, express, tracked).

The success of intermodal transportation depends on high efficiency, high system capacity, and the use of terminals brought up to a high-tech intermodal level. During the last quarter of a century, intermodal enthusiasts have worked toward erasing the obstacles of inefficient intermodal facilities at U.S. ports, truck-rail transfer points throughout the nation, and major connecting nodes among carriers. Five million containers are in transit globally at any one moment.

HOPE

How does intermodal transportation fit into an intelligent logistics infrastructure in the U.S.? In the last few decades, intermodal specialists have tried to iron out the obstacles of inefficient intermodal facilities. The new intermodal yards, such as the one planned by CSX at Winter Haven, Florida, for instance, have been planned and designed to take intermodal processing to the new high-tech levels. Carmichael points out that in Meridian, Mississippi, the improvements to the Kansas City Southern/Norfolk Southern "Meridian Speedway" have created a transportation corridor of national importance.

It is hard to think of rail as a future solution. This may be why rail gets a short supply of good press, or any press at all. The average railroader keeps a very low profile in an era of high profiles. They think as railroaders and not as transporters. The younger people coming into rail may think differently. Certainly they will think in digital terms as they are used to computers and software programs as means to run things with automation and, when necessary, quite remotely from their physical function.

3PLS AND COLLABORATION

Many 3PLs now provide Web services that bring together various modes of transportation. They are most often not owners of equipment (trucks, railroads, or aircraft), so their success depends to some extent on the level of efficiency of each mode of transportation chosen by them for their customers and the intermodal opportunities as they move through the supply chain.

A company such as Cogistics, Inc. of Lakeland, Florida, has made that possible by building a large data warehouse and a secure Web portal to offer a broadly based service. It includes online shipping visibility, carriers, and choice of route and timing of route as well as freight bill pre-audit and carrier payment processing. It works with many U.S. companies, such as tier 1 suppliers to Ford and GM who ship many parts and components to Mexico for assembly.

The 3PLs assist with inbound shipments that can be very complex. They may use their preferred shippers and Cogistics in a collaborative arrangement that they manage, and they can expedite the complexity of dealing with the road system in Mexico. They can, for instance, increase the capacity of each shipment by truck by a large percentage and give the supplier an advantage that can go right to the bottom line.

Logistic Collaboration Solutions (LCS), from Oakscape of Tampa, also offers logistics solutions in a Web-based wireless format. It has organized these as five interrelated modules: shipment visibility, problem resolution, carrier performance, decision support, and a wireless interface. Its solution gives multiple views into transportation transactions and allows users the opportunity to be in charge of transportation execution and real-time decision changes.

Another 3PL, Nistevo Corporation of Eden Prairie, Minnesota, offers a different collaborative logistics network that includes over

400 carriers. It analyzes collaborative logistics in three basic forms of collaboration: shipper to carrier, shipper to shipper, and supplier to retailer to carrier. In each case, concentration is on different aspects of the process. In shipper to carrier, for instance, the focus is on the contract management between the collaborators and also the ability to track and communicate execution using its system.

WEB SOLUTIONS

As more and more vendors move to Web-based solutions for their customers, the choices are increasing for an enterprise that wants to move toward solving collaborative logistics problems. Some enterprise software vendors such as IFS and SAP have moved from an enterprise resource planning (ERP) world into providing logistics and supply chain solutions that are portal based, and have the strength of deep experience in business solutions. The traditional ERP providers are moving into the supply chain.

Solving visibility problems, overcapacity, empty loads, and bad bookings may need a kick start of a very real commitment to the collaborative process, and this means being open to working with other entities. Collaborative logistics is built one trust at a time. It could be wished that the infrastructure within which logistics operates were organized in a fully collaborative manner. But it is not.

UNEVEN RAILS

Rail worldwide is a mixed bag. In Europe and Japan, there is great respect for the railroads, and railroads are generally good. The United States started big, got deregulated, and went smaller and nearly gasped out. The railroads are now entering the electronic era, having weathered a long bout with the effects of deregulation. U.S. railroads haul 25 percent of all freight. As of 2004, there were 1.2 million freight cars in use, operated by a workforce of over 175,000.

The railroads have made the transition from steam power to diesel power, from large railroad crews to now most likely two-person trains. Small cars have given way to larger and longer cars (from 40-foot box cars to 50-foot cars, and flat cars now able to hold two 53-foot containers, for instance).

One company, CSX Intermodal, makes use of advanced technology tools such as a radio frequency system that wirelessly connects personal computers to its cranes, hostlers (railroad moving personnel), and supervisor vehicles to its terminal operating system. This gives those using the system real-time reporting of the intermodal shipping process. CSX is also a user of an Internet-based EDI system that allows its customers to submit bills of lading, check on their shipment status, and transfer funds electronically as well as receive freight billing.

Some U.S. railroads are moving ahead to a degree, and are able to earn the cost of capital for the first time since deregulation. You might ask what makes railroads different than the trucks on highways and aircraft in air lanes. Railroads own their own right of way. The airlines, containerships, and the truck fleets don't. Railroading is a capital-intensive business. There are few alternative uses for the rails.

RAIL GAINS

There have been some productivity gains in the industry, according to the Association of American Railroads (AAR). The railroads experienced the greatest productivity gains in history when they went from the 100-mile day for crews, five-person crews, low-horsepower locomotives, and small cars to what we have today: largely two-person crews and high-horsepower locomotives. In 1970, there were about one million workers. Today the railroads are handling more gross tonnage annually than ever before, with between 125,000 and 135,000 people.

The challenge now is what to do next after having had large gains through engine enhancement, the transfer from large to small crews, an increase in car size, and stack cars. You can go from a two-person crew to a one-person crew or even, with telematics (for instance, GPS, handheld computers, bar code scanners, etc.), to a no-person crew. That will be a gain in productivity, but these gains will be more incremental than the huge gains of the recent past.

KEEP ON TRUCKING

Let's also consider trucking. There are 2.7 million tractor trailer trucks and over 3 million truck drivers on U.S. roads, and they buy 51.4 billion gallons of fuel (diesel and gasoline) per year. Trucking hauls something close to 70 percent of all U.S. freight tonnage. This amounts to 10.7 billion tons of freight, and the amount of material being hauled continues to rise.

In 2006, trucking companies spent $102 billion on diesel fuel. This constitutes a rise from $88 billion the previous year. The figure is double what it was four years ago. Fuel has been traditionally the second most expensive cost of trucking, but is quickly catching up to labor as the number one expense.

There are 600,000-plus trucking companies, and 96 percent of them have fewer than 20 trucks. For some of these companies, the cost of fuel may have already exceeded labor. This is not true of the industry as a whole. Drivers' wages have been going up as well.

Smaller trucking companies don't have the buying power for fuel purchases that some of their larger counterparts do. However, the industry has not seen the number of failures as it did during past fuel hikes, and increasingly prevalent fuel surcharges may be one of the reasons. It is a tool that truck companies can use to pass along the costs. Those costs can eventually be passed on to the consumer. It seems the industry would not have its present survival rate without the surcharge. The downside is the fact that because truckers are spending so much more money on fuel, they can't spend on other items that might be the order of the day such as advanced technology (telematics).

The need for infrastructure improvement to move the economy forward and help the trucking industry is a primary mission of the American Trucking Association. From 1980 to 2000, there was a 100 percent increase in truck mileage and a 61 percent increase in the number of trucks on the road. During this time, however, there was only a 3 percent increase in the roads available for truck transportation.

The situation in developing countries is far more dire, as trucks lack regulation, equipment is often old, drivers are untrained, and the infrastructure—in the form of unpaved roads, narrow bridges, poor culvert maintenance, and lack of road shoulder repair—adds to the fact that few trucks are parts of fleets and lack electronic communication and control.

SUMMING UP: TRANSPORTATION

We have reviewed the major transport methods in the United States (and, to some extent, abroad) and some of their strengths and weaknesses. The competition is keen. The need worldwide for better infrastructures and more equitable allotment of goods regionally and nationally has been acknowledged. The growing dominance of Asia in ports, container handling, and shipping has been noted. If you want to improve transport, it would be best to start with better allocation of world funding for balanced and improved transport infrastructure. We all gain if transportation becomes more efficient and more equitable.

Chapter 15

A MILLION SQUARE FEET OF CHOCOLATE: WAREHOUSING AND DISTRIBUTION CENTERS

Warehousing, sorting, and distributing are both architecture and methodology. They may be a central key to a good supply network. The position of a distribution center is as critical as its size and the level of its technology. If the warehouse serves many retail stores, it should be located at the shortest set of routes to the stores as possible, with consideration for the road infrastructure. If the distribution center serves a set of manufacturing plants, then the type of manufacturing proximity to air, truck, and rail become of top consequence. The warehouse and distribution center is where demand hits the road. The switch from warehouses to distribution centers is a natural evolution from the need for reduced cost of transportation and materials handling and the move away from storage.

A TRUCK DOCKING WORLD

What can be more than 10 times larger than a football field? What is most often located in a rural setting, and acts as the lifeblood of a retailer, a manufacturer, or the U.S. defense system? It is a modern distribution center. Distribution centers (DCs) are often 1,000,000 square feet in area and several stories tall.

DCs have been placed in recent years in rural settings. That is where the space is and where the cost of purchase can be contained. These locations also may be easier to access than an urban or suburban location. They can be recognized most easily by the nearly endless truck-loading docks on all sides. Ten years ago, a DC may have been half this size or far smaller. Distribution centers now represent a new way of thinking in logistics, one that makes a virtue out of just-in-time goods and products processing.

Distribution centers and warehousing are more doors than walls in order to have minimum length to carry goods internally. So the buildings are recognizable by their frequent portals. Storing of goods is a warehouse's and, to a degree, a distribution center's function, but storage is not value added. Dead storage is bad business.

Sorting is a major function of both warehouses and distribution centers. The sorting can be of many varieties: by type of goods, by an order required, by date as in perishable goods, or by value or as goods in a bonded condition. More sophisticated sorting and handling can lead to refashioning and repacking, remanufacturing, and redistributing.

Distribution centers are embraced as a solution to satisfying the demand of customers for the right goods at the right time at the right cost. The distribution center today is an outward manifestation of an inner change in logistics.

IN AND OUT

Distribution centers have some aspects of warehouses, because they can receive and distribute goods and also can hold them, but not to the degree of a warehouse. They are essentially exchange centers. Goods come in one loading dock and can go directly out of another to a different truck. The truckload more often is broken down into various pallets and redistributed to a number of loading docks. Then the load goes on other trucks for broader distribution.

As the goods pass within the distribution center they are barcoded and thereby recorded as to what is being shipped, where it has been, and when it passed through a given point. Or they are given an RFID treatment using wireless technology and advanced sensor designs. They are then sent on their way as scheduled and recorded by a logistics or warehouse software application. This process assures the supplier, the retailer, or manufacturer of what has arrived where and what is going out, in real time. The value that is associated with this real-time process is that everyone gets the same information when tuning in at the same time. This means one sharable record, and less room for error. Such information, such as estimated time of arrival, can be checked against actual time of arrival.

NOT A CRYSTAL BALL YET

As RFID takes hold in the future, a wealth of information will be available about a given pallet of goods, package of goods, or raw material. The world is not there yet. We can see the possibilities, but there are many shadows that fall across our path. Right now there are too many unmarked items, too many needs, too many mistakes, too many unreliable installations of even good hardware and software, and the cost of full tracking could be staggering. Only great results will justify such an investment.

BEYOND STORAGE

What are distribution centers, and direct delivery that does not need even a distribution center, replacing? They are, to a great extent, replacing warehouses. They are replacing warehouse facilities that acted as quasi-distribution centers and in-house warehouse or storage facilities for manufacturing or wholesaling. The reason for this is multifold. Warehouses have traditionally stored goods in anticipation of when and if they are needed.

Unfortunately for those paying the price of maintaining inventory in a warehouse, there is a high cost to inventory. It has no value added sitting on a shelf. It may be nice to have the knowledge of what is there using a warehouse management software, but the knowledge does not pay the storage bill. Warehouses need not be static, but they were originally designed to store goods, not to process them rapidly.

OVER ONE MILLION SQUARE FEET OF CHOCOLATE

The increase in size of distribution centers, such as the relatively new 1.2 million square foot Hershey Foods DC in Hershey, Pennsylvania, is a reflection of either a manufacturer's need or a retailer's need. There are more products and more forms of each product.

A trip through The Home Depot will, as well, remind us of the fecundity of types of products of various scales and complexities. All this calls for larger and larger centers. The increase in the number of centers is a reflection of more stores, more competition, a larger population, and the need for better logistical service to retailing, wholesaling, and manufacturing.

However, let's get back to a customer or consumer view of all this activity, and look at the subject of return of merchandise, or reverse logistics.

REVERSE LOGISTICS

We all suffer when we have to return something—the consumer, the store, and the manufacturer. The business of returns starts when a customer, retailer, dealer, or manufacturer finds something wrong with a product (outdated, spoiled, broken, or flawed). This discovery should initiate a response that, through appropriate automation, takes care of responsibility assignment, return transportation, returns information data and physical processing, eventual redistribution or recycling, and compensation to the customer.

Reverse logistics can be painful, time consuming, and costly for all involved: manufacturer, retailer, and customer. They may be best known to consumers as those long product return lines at stores during the holidays, or by the news that their Ford Explorer has just been recalled. Returns and recalls are part of a supply chain.

In 2004, the cost of reverse logistics was $58.34 billion in the United States alone. This represents one-half of 1 percent of the GDP. 3PLs are a vital link in delivering solutions to reverse logistics costs and returns processing.

TWO VIEWS

Donald Maltby, executive director of Unyson Logistics, a 3PL, sees a way toward a return on investment (ROI) in the application of reverse logistics. This means turning what can be a large deficit, and a nuisance to the store and the customer into profit. If a company looks into the costs associated with handling its own returns program, it has to invent from the outset. The benefit of utilizing a 3PL solution is that it can be already set up to manage ROI in returns and reverse logistics. The factors that have to be controlled if they go it alone include cost of labor, lack of process and supply chain visibility, and increased costs of internal administration. Maltby describes his reverse logistics application as a solution that allows vendors, suppliers, and clients to see open orders (and purchase orders) throughout the supply chain. They accomplish this with Internet-based decision support and logistics management tools. The benefit goes to the bottom line and that is good news.

Joan Starkowsky, president of Reverse Logistics, sees reverse logistics as part of product life cycle management, which is the soup-to-nuts evolution of a product from inception to design, engineering, manufacture, packaging, marketing, sales, and feedback from the customer. Return management should be considered up front as part of product development marketing. This is not always the case, and it results in a form of chaotic reaction and cost. If they are thought out and planned for, a store's returns can be a benefit: an opportunity for better customer relationships, containment of cost, profitable growth, and critical customer product feedback.

Starkowsky believes in improving profit outcomes by preventing unnecessary returns. For instance, when returns are not monitored, companies issue millions of dollars in return credits for nonprogram products (products that are not theirs). It causes a negation at the bottom line. Monitoring, according to Starkowsky, can cut up to 30 percent in credit issuance. For example, this can be transportation costs. These costs can be reduced through shipping efficiencies such as catching nonprogram products or products that can be disposed of before being trucked. Quality is best done at the beginning, and an effective returns program requires a plan at all levels ahead of the fact of the return.

GOING IN REVERSE

Here are a few suggestions for those facing reverse logistics cost or processing problems. First, the outsourcing of reverse logistics to a third-party logistics provider may be the wisest choice. A 3PL is at this business all year long, and intensely. It is a major service that they can provide. Whatever pain there may be in the process of reverse logistics can be passed on to the 3PL, allowing a company to concentrate on its core business. Second, success in the reverse logistics process depends on higher visibility of selective information and as close to real-time process knowledge as possible. The reverse logistics process is a vital connection to a company's consumer; satisfaction in the process may be a key to maintaining the customer's loyalty. Third, a smart reverse logistics system can prevent the cost of processing returns that are not actually the responsibility of the manufacturer, and prevent useless transportation before it begins. There is little or no point to providing a service for which the company is not responsible. If the warranty has passed its date, if the item does not have a legal paper trail, the company should have a means of knowing that. Last, keep the process simple for all involved. The reverse logistics process is usually thought of as a negative and is slotted into the cost column. If looked at creatively, it can be a mechanism for renewed customer loyalty and increased sales.

SUMMING UP: WAREHOUSING AND DISTRIBUTION

Distribution centers and warehouses are where the rubber gets off the road and goods are sorted and re-sent (hopefully quickly). They represent in their moving belts, automatic sorters, bar code readers, and RFID the place where the supply chains logistics action is at white heat. They are where a UPS or a Wal-Mart makes a big difference in synchronized supply. They are a vital midpoint between the manufacturer and the customer. They allow for a state of efficiency that permits and encourages delivering well to a customer (of one, if that is what is required).

Part Three

SUPPLY CHAIN RESOLUTION

Now let's look at what we may have missed or done wrong in the development of new logistics practices, the supply chain and its strategies, and the supporting infrastructure that has so far made it all possible. The emergence of China, along with its opportunities and problems, is considered from an analyst's point of view. Then we'll look at a sequence of solutions or suggested solutions for modeling the supply chain, starting with W. Edwards Deming and ending with an organic perspective on the supply chain. Finally, I'll cover several recommendations for repairing our world's supply chain and its infrastructure, and recommend a logistics and supply chain focus that acts in an organic way with intelligent response to customer demand.

Chapter

16

WHAT'S MISSING? SUPPLY CHAIN CHALLENGES

The United States has gone from a position of logistical and manufacturing strength to a position of vulnerability. Logistics goes beyond our simple definition. It has its origins. Let's get closer to the meaning of the supply chain. These concepts and practices affect business today in large measure as they move through the worlds of transport, retailing, and manufacture. China has become a manufacturing superproducer. How did these things come to pass, and where are Europe and the rest of the world in all of this?

A PROCLIVITY TO BE WRONG

One of the hallmarks of a civilization is the predilection to predict. The prediction of where a technology or service is going is fraught with complications and errors.

Thomas Watson, the original chairman of IBM, is said to have remarked in 1943 that he thought there was a world market for maybe five computers. Watson lived to see IBM mass producing the

360 computer and many others. Along the same lines, a statement in 1949 *Popular Mechanics* forecasted, that computers in the future might weigh no more than 1.5 tons.

An IBM engineer in 1968 wondered what in the world the microchip was good for. It is reassuring that the engineer was at an advanced facility. "There is no reason for any individual to have a computer in his home," "Ken Olsen, president of Digital Equipment Corporation, remarked in 1977. These days, it might be better to have two or three if the kids want to log on too. "64K ought to be enough memory for anybody," according to Bill Gates, later chairman of Microsoft, in 1981.

WHY?

Why is U.S. discrete manufacturing so weak and retailing so strong? Why is the infrastructure so bad and yet carriers such as UPS, FedEx, and DHL so strong? Two and a half million truck drivers are trying to deliver goods, but they do not have the roads they need.

Why is the infrastructure of a city, a state, or a nation of the world a factor? What is global trade doing to the United States? How does technology fit into this? More to the point, what processes, things, or systems need to be upgraded to make U.S. businesses, and the nation, more productive? Let's start with the beginnings of logistics and the supply chain.

ROADS

For now, forget the ports. What about the roads? We already know that the United States' interstate system of highways is almost beyond repair, having remained nearly static for 50 years. The highway system comprises 1 percent of the U.S. road system, and yet handles 24 percent of the nation's traffic.

There is no federal plan in place for its replacement or improvement; for that matter, there is no plan of any kind in place either.

Roads carry trucks, trucks carry goods, trucks guzzle lots of fuel, and fuel prices are off the chart. Weaknesses in the infrastructure have very real effects on the supply chain.

AIRPORTS

The United States has not built any new airports in over 13 years, and has built few new runways at existing airports. This is accompanied by poor on-time performance by airlines nationwide. Most of the country's air carriers are suffering financially or are in bankruptcy. There are a few exceptions such as Southwest and, of course, the commercial freight carriers UPS, FedEx, and DHL. The foreign air carriers are, for the most part, subsidized, or they too would be flying through red ink.

RAILS

The United States has an almost nonexistent passenger rail system compared to Europe and Japan. After deregulation, the existing freight rail companies closed down tracks and only very recently have added any tracks at all. In 1970, the United States had close to 1.5 million rail vehicles. As of 2002, that number was down to 500,000. In 1916, there were around 245,000 miles of track in the United States, and now Class 1 railroads operate, albeit more efficiently, over about 120,000 miles of track.

INTERMODAL AGAIN

There are insufficient intermodal facilities, and inadequate technology application to U.S. rail yards, for train-to-truck and truck-to-train transfer. The railroads move ahead by private means alone, while China's railroads go ahead with full support from the government.

As U.S. businesses outsource manufacturing, they concentrate on competitive supply chains that—for better or worse—depend on a strong internal and foreign transportation and logistics infrastructure that are foreign-controlled.

THE CHINA CARD

China positioned itself as a major piece of the supply chain world. It is important with any discussion of the nature of the supply chain because of its size, the growth of its manufacturing business, and its growing economic and transportation position. Doing business in China may be an ever more vital part of tomorrow's economic reality for better or worse.

Within a more than $2 trillion GDP, the fourth largest in the world, China is becoming not just the world's manufacturer but also the supply chain king. The first quarter of 2006 saw an overall growth of 10.3 percent over the same period in 2005. In 2004, China exported $593.4 billion in goods while importing $561.4 billion. This is a far better balance of trade than the United States: In 2005, the United States exported $34.7 billion to China while China exported to the United States $196.6 billion.

China's major ports that conduct the bulk of its trade are Shanghai, Hong Kong, and Shenzhen. Together they handle more than 55 million shipping containers a year. The length of the Great Wall of China is impressive; however, these shipping containers laid end to end would girdle one quarter of the circumference of the Earth.

However, airfreight is accounting for more and more of China's high-tech products transport and some other more sensitive or costly goods, such as high fashions. The Anchorage Economic Development Council expects China's air business to continue to grow by 10 percent each year for the next 20 years. According to Bob Poe, its CEO, Anchorage Airport has more Asian air cargo than anyone and lands the most cargo of any airport in the United States.

Another consequence of growth is the growing need for warehouse space, and the problems of increased inventories and longer supply lines. There is a move in China toward adopting warehouse management system (WMS) software to accommodate these needs and help the bottom line. Warehousing is a growth business, as recent expansion by one company, ProLogis, indicates. ProLogis is planning new distribution parks in Quindao, Hangzhou, and Ningbo (all coastal cities) that comprise three million square feet of space. Companies such as Wal-Mart have their own growth pattern in China; having first opened there in 1996, the company has 56 store units and is the single largest buyer of Chinese products. It has been noted that if Wal-Mart were a country, it would rank eighth in the list of China's world trading partners.

LOGISTICS DON'T COME CHEAP

China's logistics costs for 2004 were $351.6 billion (in U.S. dollars). These costs have increased appreciably since then. Over 20 percent of China's GDP is spent on logistics, as opposed to over 8 percent for the United States. However, the percentage has started to come down, indicating an improvement in the country's logistic operations. Part of its costs involves substantial toll costs on toll roads, and far too many trucking companies (small fleets or single trucks) that do not have the efficiency of scale. China invested $87.8 billion in logistics infrastructure in 2004, 83 percent of which was for transportation improvements. Over the next 15 years, the Chinese government plans to build 50,000 kilometers of expressways. Chinese businesses pay more to move goods than their U.S. counterparts, partly because their roads are still not adequate for their growing needs. China's gaps in transportation (road and rail principally) and its shortfall in logistics (tracking, customs handling) hamper its profits, if not its efficiency.

China is clearly the place to do business for many. The three major economic regions consist of: the Bahai Sea River (Beijing), the Yangtze River Delta (Shanghai), and the Pearl River (Guangzhou and Hong Kong). They are the principal engines fuelling China's economy, and they are fed their energy in the form of coal from the west of China. The enormous increase in manufacturing has consequently hobbled the Chinese environment with a great pollution problem in the air, water, and ground. The growth of manufacturing has also made China a predominant industrial contender.

TAXI TO THE RESCUE

Rick D. Blasgen, president and CEO of Council of Supply Chain Management Professionals (CSCMP), suggests that China's still-developing logistics infrastructure was what hit him the hardest. For instance, when in China, he saw perishable "frozen" foods being delivered in a taxicab.

China still has room for growth in general logistics and supply chain knowledge, a deeper understanding of third-party issues, and providing services to build supply chain networks. Mediation of disputes in China is not conducted by the same set of rules as in the United States and Europe. However, with its emergence into the arena of the World Trade Organization (WTO), China is bound to change some of its ways and reflect more closely the commitments of the WTO and its regulations.

As part of its progress, China has become the world's third largest research and development performer, according to the Organization for Economic Co-operation & Development. By 2003, China was spending $84.6 billion on R&D. China's manufacturing production is closing in on a trillion dollars, a figure that was expected to outrank the United States by the end of 2006, according to the Centre D'Etudes Prospectives Et D'Informations Internationales.

Manufacturing is often a gauge of industrial/political dominance. China is already the number one producer of steel; it is also a major player in cement, tractors, cloth, telephones, microcomputers, automobiles, and color TV sets, to name but a few. China's industrial growth rate hovers around more than 10 percent a year, while the rate of the United States is below 1 percent. The trend is unmistakably in China's favor and by a wide margin.

In China, manufacturing happens in places such as "Sock City," or Zhuji, and in "Shoe City," or Jinjiang. The figures are staggering. In Jinjiang, there are 3,000 enterprises devoted to shoe production, where 350,000 workers make 700 million pairs of shoes a year.

Michael Topolovac, the CEO of Arena Solutions, says that his clients who do business in China are facing a heavy global competitive environment. One of the major shifts his customers have seen over the last 10 years is competing not just with much better funded larger companies, but also on a global scale. On top of this, they have seen their product development cycles reduced from years to months, and time-in-market life cycles reduced as well. This sometimes is as dramatic as going from five years down to five months. All of this is happening with increasing downward price pressure. In order to compete in this environment, companies are looking to employ extended supply chains that gain them both leverage and cost advantages. To a degree, these mid-market companies are realizing that it is important for their supply chains to compete just as much as their products compete.

Topolovac suggests that this led many companies to look to China as a key part of their manufacturing strategies. A vast majority of the companies we see today are either currently outsourcing to China or intend to do so in the near future. Despite its many benefits, it is not a move without significant business challenges. Two frequent challenges are the lack of communication and IT infrastructure, and the protection of intellectual property.

Doing business in China is never less than challenging as social, political, and economic forces change the landscape along with the smog. The Chinese will, in time, take care of the smog as they continue to convert from coal to oil and other energy sources. This will probably encourage further growth in internal and international supply chain activity—but at a cost to the Earth.

ANALYSTS' VIEWS

Part of becoming a major manufacturer and a nation of consumers is the dreadful increase in production of trash. China now produces 190 million tons of trash a year, outdistancing even the United States. This is just one aspect of pollution facing China. The air in many of the manufacturing regions is notoriously bad. Another factor that impacts heavily on Chinese logistics is the cost of moving goods through the many road tolls. Trucking a 40-foot container from Beijing to Shanghai, about 900 miles, can cost as much as $400 in tolls (along toll roads). The alternative is to travel on non–toll roads and encounter endless congestion.

There are many advantages that induce companies not just to stay in China, but to increase their presence. Mark Hillman, the research director of AMR Research, suggests that China has become an integral part of the supply chain strategy of a large number of companies. Thinking about the role of sourcing from China has matured in a significant way. Two or three years ago, it was almost a knee-jerk reaction for companies to say that their competitors were sourcing from China and that they must do the same or be unable to compete. Many companies did not apply much thought to the management of China-based manufacturing or the total cost implications of China-sourced goods. The major impacts of China sourcing are increases both in lead times and in lead-time variability, which often has the result of needing to create more inventories at various levels of the supply chain to act as a buffer against increased variability. Such an activity, according to Hillman, eats away at the cost benefits of the procured supply.

It is critical to find a way to take advantage of local knowledge (cultural and intellectual). This is certainly one of the major challenges, as the ranks of experienced Chinese middle managers are not as plentiful as is the current need for them. Many companies choose to relocate a few critical employees to China to help manage processes and collaboration on the ground. The issue of language can be more than trivial; unlike in India, there is not a tradition of learning English as a second language.

The common success factors of firms that have reaped tangible benefit from conducting business in China include:

- Taking a strategic look at the China opportunity. It's not just about sourcing cheaper goods; it's about thinking longer term about China's role as a consumer of foreign-branded, locally manufactured products.
- Taking a total-cost view of China sourcing is critical to leveraging the expected savings and returns.
- Understanding the various types of structures for doing business in China, such as joint-venture structures and wholly owned subsidiary structures, to understand the tax treatment impacts and other structural advantages and disadvantages.
- Considering a segmentation strategy for sourcing is also critical, and hybrid approaches are often the best strategy. For example, for products with stable demand patterns, China sourcing is a great option because of the longer lead times and stable replenishment demand patterns. However, products with highly variable demand are not normally great candidates for China sourcing, unless they have a very high value-to-weight ratio, which makes the occasional use of airfreight a viable option.

Adrian Gonzalez, a research director at the ARC Advisory Group, has two kinds of China success stories to offer. In terms of having the most experience working in China, Caterpillar (over 80 years) and Volkswagen (since 1984) are good examples. Being "early to market" enabled Volkswagen to establish a strong brand and gain market share in the country, but the company is struggling a bit these days as lower-priced competitors, both domestic and foreign (e.g., Hyundai), have emerged.

Yum! Brands is another China success story. KFC and Pizza Hut are the two most recognizable brands in China according to a

Nielsen survey, and ahead of other brands such as Coke and Nike. The company opened over 400 new units in China in 2005, bringing its total to over 2,200 restaurants. Yum! Brands derived $1.2 billion in revenues and $200 million in operating profit from China in 2005. The growth of these businesses in China can be accounted for by two major trends: the rapid emergence of a Chinese middle class and the need, particularly in cities, for organized fast food service.

GROWTH

Gonzalez feels that, in general, growth will come from industries where China significantly lags behind the West and/or those that are critical to long-term economic growth and social stability. Logistics certainly falls into these categories. China's logistics costs as a percent of GDP are about double what they are in the United States.

The pharmaceutical industry is another important industry for China, considering its large and aging population. China is now investing to modernize the pharmaceutical industry and its health care distribution network.

Finally, although its economic growth has led to environmental concerns, the country's leaders do realize that it must take action, or else China (with its huge population and limited developable land, bad air, and poor water) will ultimately become the world's largest garbage dump. Therefore, remanufacturing (i.e., reclaiming parts from used automobiles, machinery, and high-tech equipment) is sure to become a growth area in the years to come.

WHAT GOES?

Finally, Gonzalez notes that doing business in China is not always the lowest-cost or best option for your supply chain. For example, if "speed to market" is more critical than cost, local sourcing and production may be better. The same thinking applies to many new product introductions, especially for a first-of-a-kind product that can face quality issues in the near term. It is easier and faster to replace products and resolve quality issues when manufacturing is performed locally (as opposed to having to deal across time zones and foreign languages). If a company goes to China, it is vital to have local resources that can help it navigate through the web of regulations and differences in cultural norms.

PLAQUE IN THE WORLD'S ARTERIES

Plaque has built up in the world's logistics and transportation arteries. Many other parts of the world are inadequately served logistically. Transport by road outside of Europe is often questionable when measured by the standards of just-in-time delivery. Africa has inadequate rail, roads, airports, sea ports, and stability but plenty of graft. The only great sea ports are in South Africa. India's ports, roads, and rails are overtaxed and underdeveloped. The Indian government lacks control of its system and also has to contend with graft. India is becoming the software center of the world within a nation that lacks even the minimum of infrastructure for moving and handling goods. China's inadequate roads are overcontrolled by graft, but the country's general thrust toward an improved infrastructure is impressive.

The Panama Canal presents another challenge. It is grossly inadequate in width, depth, and lock technology. Only the "little ships" go through the locks. As the older, smaller ships are scrapped, the canal will ccase to be functional.

STRESS DRIVEN

At the turn of the 20th century, market stress on the need for automobiles pushed Ford, and soon others, into mass production. Later, the stress of Sputnik led to a new rule set for the United States that translated into miniaturization, computerization, connectivity, and visibility of elements. More recently, the advent of the World Wide Web and its attendant communication revolution in networking has led manufacturing into collaboration, software downloading, and supply chain management on a grand scale.

Some of the supply chain, logistics, and manufacturing stress-driven rule set changes are as follows: going from mass production to custom to one-off; going from islands of automation to integrated automation; going from sneaker-net to Ethernet to Internet; going from warehouse clipboards to computerized relational databases, from quality checks at the end to quality at the beginning and all the way through, from unaccountable production to compliance, from discontinuous logistics to the supply chain, and from made-to-stock to made-to-order.

SUMMING UP: WORLD SUPPLY CHAINS JUST HAPPEN

What I am saying is not a planned economy recommendation. But it is a recommendation for a responsive process. There is much wrong and much missing. The real issue is creating a priority of values as they are reflected in making certain vital decisions. These decisions have to result in action, not in more words and plans or study commissions. The hard part today is making a transfer from a vision to realization. If you want greater accountability, prepare for far greater responsibility.

Chapter

17

PYRAMIDS TO PARAMECIUMS: SUPPLY CHAIN MODELING

Modeling is a technique of taking the shape and relationship of a process or a thing that is an approximation of the nature of the actual process or thing. It is always an approximation. Like an outline, it is not fully narrative, nor descriptive, but it is useful in presenting a brief overview. The execution of an ideal model is the hard part; the complex realities of the supply chain are not easily put into a model.

Seeing complexity simply is a difficult art. It is possible to create a very bad model. Being able to model does not assure success in modeling. For instance, there are limits to the meanings of intersecting circles in a Venn diagram. One of the big troubles is that you may start believing that their intersections reflect reality. These grandchildren of logic diagrams can be very misinforming. There are also limits to XYZ charts as models. An XYZ chart shows values in space along three dimensions. They may serve engineering because so much is analyzable in an XYZ context. There are limits to bar charts. Company organizational charts are another dead end, because the charts reflect management's perception of the structure, and the structure may be totally different.

DEMING MODEL

The model of the supply chain or manufacturing network began with W. Edwards Deming, who first conceptualized the idea of production viewed as a system. He defined the not-yet-named supply chain as a product of gradualism, long-term commitment, and a measured and intelligent application of quality processes. He believed that if you can't describe what you are doing with a process, you don't know what you are doing. Let me outline his basic thesis.

1. He saw the customer as the most important part of the production line. The customer was at the end of the line, which he defined starting at suppliers and going through production and distribution.
2. He saw quality as a determinant of management.
3. He saw the need for a long-term relationship with a company's customers, and with customers' customers .
4. He saw suppliers as partners with whom there would be continuous effort to improve the quality of materials and components. He saw the need to reduce variation in the quality of materials supplied.
5. He saw a chain reaction from the improvement of processes.
6. He saw the need for cooperation and trust between companies.
7. He saw the need for continuous development within organizations of respect and trust.

These ideas, when implemented, changed Japanese manufacturing and delivery to the wondrous system it is today. Deming saw the passing of materials, components, and subassemblies from one station (machine, machine/human, or human) to another as a chain that added value. It is worth noting that decades later, Michael Porter built his idea of a value chain on much the same model (he used more modern terms such as inbound logistics, operations, outbound logistics, marketing and sales, and service). A value chain by Porter's standards are processes or handoffs that provide a financial benefit, as opposed to events and processes that either don't provide a profit or result in actual losses.

In other words, one party or machine passes to another, and at each step, an increase in value is performed.

THE ALLEN-BRADLEY PYRAMID

Pyramids have been all too popular as a model of a corporation. The Allen-Bradley pyramid model was accepted almost without reservation for decades. The model from top to bottom is referred to as management control relationship: corporate/financial on top, plant on the next tier below, areas (as in manufacturing lines) below those, cells below the areas, and work units last.

It really made no sense, but it looked sensible, rather like an army model of command from the top down. The basic problem with this model is that most information dealing with the nature of a business process resides at the bottom level, while the top level may be too distant to evaluate what is going on remotely. This has been borne out in reengineering of companies. Those nearest to a process must be consulted when changes to the process are being considered. The top down approach to modeling needs to be turned upside down or discarded completely.

COMPUTER INTEGRATED MANUFACTURING MODEL

The grandfather of all subsequent manufacturing and supply chain models is computer integrated manufacturing (CIM). CIM came to pass as an idea in the late 1960s along with the introduction of the first industrial robots. Computer control had entered the factory with early applications of manufacturing resource planning (MRP) and the early developments of computer-aided design and drafting. It was, and to an extent still is, an effort to integrate what were called the "smokestacks": planning, engineering design, manufacturing control, and factory automation. It was popular, but difficult, as it took early computing technology and tried to apply it to complex and often recalcitrant processes that were full of departmental rules and obligations. Breaking down walls between departments is very hard, but to put the pieces back together again as an integrated system is even harder.

One software methodology called manufacturing resource planning (MRP), and its child, MRPII, tried to make it all work. Manufacturing resource planning in its original form incorporated capacity planning, ordering, and scheduling. Its grown up version added modules, if not real functionality. Many companies that bought into MRP found themselves using only a fraction of its offerings. About 15 percent use was common; the rest was rejected either as too complex or as less than cost effective, or because of the lack of skilled operators. MRP became in turn the prototype of enterprise resource planning (ERP). At each level of growth, these sets of control and planning functions took in more and more territory. However, ERP is less a model than a collection. It spans digitally enhanced systems that go all the way from human resources to production and capacity planning, and now to an involvement with the supply chain.

CIM, MRP, and ERP grew out of manufacturing, not out of concern for the customer. The primary concern was profit to the manufacturer based on manufacturing performance, which was to a great extent being achieved through accurate capacity planning. Perhaps manufacturers who put great stock in CIM and ERP people should have listened to Deming earlier.

AMR RESEARCH'S DEMAND MODEL

The supply chain has advanced from a tentative theory in the 1980s to furious activity and the SCOR model in the 1990s. More and more companies, both in North America and abroad, have bought in. For some businesses, the supply chain has become the key to their strategic advantage or to the development of such an advantage.

Bruce Richardson is the chief research officer at AMR Research and has contributed to the development of its demand driven supply network (DDSN). It is essentially a shift in focus from internal factors to the external demand of the customer. It is also a shift from a linear supply chain model to a circular or renewing model. It is a shift from expecting demand to shaping demand. Some of the essential elements include:

- Hardware and networking system—a system that can be scaled along with software applications and databases that command business processes. The DDSN requires a system architecture that can grow and remain flexible.
- Demand—a perspective that sees demand on many levels: open to negotiating, sensing and responding to immediate demands with a high level of business acumen
- Network—reliable and pervasive standards and communication to 3PLs, buyers, designers, and contract manufacturers

The DDSN means that the company's supply chain strategy will evolve in the following sequence:

1. Reacting—a traditional site-to-site supply chain
2. Anticipating—an internally connected enterprise lacking external integration
3. Collaborating—a connected enterprise with external integration but lacking strategic control
4. Orchestrating—DDSN integration and new business growth oriented

According to Richardson, everything in the supply chain is highly fragmented and companies tend to enhance only the part of the supply chain within which they reside. The demand side is not necessarily tied to the supply side, even in great companies. The product side is now emerging, as with product lifecycle management (PLM). We need to know how to feed any new information, such as changes in demand, back into the product and into supply. We can have a closed loop replenishment system (for manufacturing or for store). A closed loop system is one that utilizes feedback (by mechanical or sensor means) to control decisions (e.g., cool down, heat up, go faster, go slower).

Richardson sees us as starting to do a better job with J-I-T and initiatives such as narrowing the time it takes to respond to demand. But he states that we are still missing lots of opportunities on the new product side, as we do not have a fully integrated way of looking at this. The AMR's demand-driven supply network model is a way of identifying the chief business processes that come from the ultimate sources of demand and shoot through the supply networks.

BACK TO OUTSOURCING

The major concerns about global outsourcing have come from the United States, and the chief concern has been that outsourcing gives business away and is a direct cause of job losses in the country.

The fact of outsourcing is by no means new to the United States. Multinational companies have been practicing it for years. The drama comes from the juxtaposition of reduced manufacturing presence in the country as outsourcing increases, most especially to Asia. Only about 10 percent of manufacturing cost is directly related to human labor, but outsourcing has not been confined to labor alone. Today client services, company intellectual capital, and many other processes and products are being outsourced. It will, in time, come down to a question of degree—as in whether to outsource human resources, market calling centers, programming, software development, and manufacturing, or at least manufacturing assembly. It is also a question of balance: how much stays at home and is reasonably handled there, and what can go abroad to the advantage of the company? Intellectual property and its control seem to be the activity and interest that is not placed in the scales offshore. All considerations have their profit side, and to the degree that accounting is treasured by a company, profit will be a player in outsourcing decisions. Lower cost labor may not offset poor quality in accounting terms, and the bottom line can require very close scrutiny in this regard.

IBM MODEL

IBM has a centralized supply chain model. Since 1996, all of the logistics within IBM have been centralized into one organization. Even within a specific country or region, all of the company's units are coordinated, having the same views, metrics, processes, and rules of engagement. With respect to suppliers, all of the IBM teams, across all brands and divisions, use the same logistic service providers. For example, IBM's units in France, along with those in the rest of Europe, all use the same vendor for surface transportation.

Their collaboration is done in a centralized and coordinated way. They don't produce anything in Germany, for instance. An IBM server may come from Poughkeepsie, New York, and another may come from Dublin, but the coordination of these several channels is centralized in control. If they are all going to customers, their network is knowledgeable. They know what shipping requirements their customers have. The system is set up so that the order drops with enough lead time to deliver it. This is all built into the system, and transit times are all negotiated in a set of spreadsheets. This allows for flexibility and avoids delays.

CENTRAL CONTROL

A master control station at IBM tracks orders, shipments, vendors, receiving, and on-time delivery. It has a centralized dashboard of indicators. The dashboard includes a series of metrics that are available to management. Managers analyze these statistics for customers and for cycle time. These metrics start from the time the order is placed and end when the product is delivered. This fits in with the integrated supply chain principle: deliver a superior end-to-end customer experience.

However, the fact that this is good for IBM does not mean that it is therefore good for all enterprises. Embracing the supply chain and activating a worldwide logistics program, as it has done, has to be taken and judged within the context of the business objectives and the strategy of a particular company.

The power and value of solid and global supply chain planning and a logistics capability is hard to argue with, however, and turning one's back may be a quick road to the demise of one's business. The attention being given to RFID is just one indication that competitiveness in business may already be essentially an ability to win within the supply chain and logistics context.

IBM'S FRONT LINE IS THE SUPPLY CHAIN

The supply chain is on the front line of business for IBM. In 2003, the integrated supply chain enabled the IBM sales force to be 20 percent more productive. The supply chain is no longer viewed as a back-room operation. It is now an integral part of IBM's strategic business model.

According to Gary Smith, the vice president of IBM global logistics businesses will become supply chain versus supply chain. Companies that are willing to rethink the role a supply chain plays in their business (from cost-cutting factor to innovation and growth) will lead business in this new era of on-demand fulfillment. Specifically, when it comes to commodity products (such as printers, ink, or paper—businesses governed by the volume of products sold, normally at low margins of profit), the supply chain could be the only difference between competitors.

The winners will be those companies that have product in stock, can ship it in 24 hours, and can deliver effectively to the customer. It is only in recent years that supply chains have been viewed strategically and in integrated terms. Based on the IBM experience, there is substantial value in transforming the supply chain components from standalone centers of competency to integrated teams. These teams have to look at processes and technology from one end to the other and back. Smith sees IBM's people as its most valuable asset. He thinks of it as a supply chain for talent: how to get the right people skills to the right place at the right time—and do it all faster and more efficiently.

A VIRTUAL SUPPLY CHAIN MODEL

Now let us get on to virtual supply. A virtual supply chain model would substitute as many actual facilities and processes as possible with co-opted ones. This can mean either renting the warehouse and distribution center, or contracting with someone to operate it for your company. This would be true of transportation, and could also mean contracting out manufacturing and packaging. Presumably the control of these activities and the intellectual property would remain with the core company; the question is just how far such a program could be pushed.

Such a model requires agility in handling a supply chain. It has become in some cases a mark of business excellence and a measure of advantage. It heralds the emergence of what is called a dynamic distribution network. This is a strategy that allows for a good match in an expanding global marketplace. Often, virtual facilities are the choice over bricks and mortar. A dynamic network seeks a solution in as close to real time as possible; this means not depending on a tried-and-true course of distribution facilities, partners, and routes. It goes for speed and efficiency at the lowest cost possible.

A dynamic distribution network in the context of today's supply chain is the result of the fact that products are being made anywhere, to be shipped anywhere. Global sourcing is forcing the emergence of the dynamic distribution center. Companies are seeking much more flexibility and agility to manage their sourcing. It's still very common for companies to detour their finished products thousands of miles away from the markets where they will ultimately be consumed, all in the name of control. Some companies are building the capability to monitor and manage the flow of goods without having it pass through a central distribution point to match supply with demand. Instead, they are using techniques such as cross-docking from supplier and service provider locations to increase the velocity of their supply chains, allowing them the ability to delay commitment of inventory until real market demand becomes apparent. A company can now ship directly from its manufacturing plants in China to the stores of its retail customers in Ohio. This can mean large airfreight bills, but freight costs may be offset by the ability to close existing distribution centers and warehouses in the United States. This is once again winning by lessening ownership or the cost of ownership.

Supply chain management, at its essence, is the management of uncertainty. It can be, for instance, the failure of a supplier to perform or a sudden change in market demand. Historically, many companies have dealt with uncertainty by using inventory and other assets as buffers. That may be a good approach when the effect of uncertainty on a business is small. When the range of uncertainty is greater, however, it becomes financially unfeasible to use this tactic.

FLEXIBILITY

Enterprises are left with other choices. They can try to eliminate the sources of uncertainty (this can translate into overdependence on one supplier or shipper or on a standard route). They can be flexible enough to change business plans quickly to accommodate uncertainty. A dynamic distribution network should mean flexibility. Through adjustment of plans and deployment of inventory at any point of the supply chain, companies can contend with uncertainty, without building huge, expensive, buffers to act as a contingency. Companies may equate flexibility with loss of control. That's because their supply chains lack the visibility of activities and events that allow them to judge the right action.

A dynamic distribution network may reduce customer uncertainty over availability and delivery, which makes a provider company more attractive to do business with. Internal operations of companies that are successful in the use of dynamic distribution networks are highly integrated. They have common performance measures that extend across the entire organization. One function does not optimize its performance at the expense of others.

INTEL'S MODEL

Intel anticipates the evolution of a more adaptive and organic model, a sensor-based network that would combine billions of sensors in intelligent self-organizing network systems—a veritable digital "nervous system."

Intel's broad product line includes CPUs, boards, chipsets, systems, and software development tools that serve as the building blocks for a great deal of advanced computing, network building, and server and communication tools. Its information architecture allows Intel to make use of RFID technology in several ways:

- Capture information from readers and sensors. Information at this level has to be filtered and consolidated.
- Manage information; a consistent and reliable view of information is essential.
- Analyze data and events in near real time to provide business intelligence and business activity monitoring.
- Access information, making it available on demand to ERP planning applications, trading partners, and customers.
- Act on information, responding to events and managing exceptions anywhere along what is now called the value chain.

For Intel, RFID enables retail supply chains and consumer-driven networks across the board in various industries.

One way to make an organic model more accessible as an actual practice would be to create new and smaller shipping containers. They would fit together in many physical combinations (long, tall, and square) and would be fully "RFIDed." These new containers would talk to whoever had access and priority. They could be picked up, loaded, shipped, unloaded, and sorted automatically. They would be both trackable and stackable.

ADAPTIVE AND ORGANIC MODEL

A simple organism is able to adapt to changes in its environment. This may mean moving, moving faster, changing dimension or configuration, modifying temperature, or reenergizing as in eating. A complex organism takes these adaptations to another level and may use tools or act differently in different media—walk on land, swim in water, soar in the air. A supply chain can be made to act more and more like an intelligent microorganism. It can adapt to changes dynamically in as close to real time as possible. This is what a dynamic distribution network is. It is what Intel espouses, and it is the direction in which businesses such as IBM, Dell, HP, Wal-Mart, and Steve & Barry's are going.

Let me use the analogy of baseball and the action of the triple play. The action of a triple play comes down most often to the infield players along with umpires that call the shots. A hit by a batter initiates the action. The ball, the key to a great deal of the action, can be caught or fielded, which translates into an "out" or the necessity of tagging out two or more runners on base. The number of permutations per situation is awesome, complicated by conditions such as running speed, the speed of throws, weather conditions, and the positions of both runners and fielders when the action breaks. Decisions have to be made about who to tag and in what sequence; these decisions are synchronous, occur at maximum speed, and demand a high level of talent and skill. Everything happens J-I-T and in seconds—or it does not happen at all. There is no time for orders from anybody. No player is subordinate to another. Independent judgment works with distributed and shared control. This is adaptive behavior at its best.

Like baseball, business needs good decision making as fast as is required to keep the business on target. Time defeats us. The way players handle a triple play is a good model for executive, staff, and worker behavior and for the support system that allows them to get the processes in hand, on time, and with quality—the three elements of the supply chain triple play. Missed timing can mean missed supply, which can mean missed manufacturing, and a missed market.

A ball team, or a business, is an interacting network of people. They can carry off a triple play only by having the capability to assess the action almost instantly, and to respond even more quickly.

AN ADAPTIVE CARRIER SYSTEM

An adaptive carrier system is one that is able to make changes while goods are in transit. This may consist of trip rerouting while the load in a truck is in transit. It may mean fast load changing as conditions change according to the demand from a central store control point. It may mean a re-sorting of goods within a distribution center based on seasonal impact, as noted by a remote source such as a buyer or a marketer. It may mean reorganizing a fleet of trucks or a train load to distribute to a whole new set of locations. It is a triple play solution at work in a system of transportation.

AN ADAPTIVE RETAILING SYSTEM

In order to be adaptive and follow an organic model, a store has to be flexible in the following ways:

- Design—replenishment of stock should be easily accomplished and customer driven. One bookstore in the Netherlands is already using RFID on books to keep track of store inventory, purchase of stock, and reorder of stock.
- Display—products can be presented as part of an environment, as in IKEA, Bloomingdales, and other department stores, or items on pallets, as at Costco. It depends on what the customer expects. Form should follow function.
- Shelf space—shelving has to have variable units. Shelf space is not storage, but point of sale. There is a big difference, even in a warehouse-style retail store. The shelves need to talk to the managers and, if possible, to the customers.
- Planning—an adaptive retailing system has to be flexible in the minds of those who plan it, run it, supervise it, and work it.

AN ADAPTIVE INFORMATION NETWORK

Alongside the sped-up processes of manufacturing and the supply chain, the attendant flow of data has increased: the data of order entry, quality control, and logistics. If we had a pause button, we could trace individual commands or orders in relation to the actual movement of goods, parts, and products.

Those who work in logistics might tend to see scheduling of air, sea, and land freight, or J-I-T delivery, or installation of a new bar code scanner as paramount; while those directly in manufacturing may well be concentrating on tool wear or boiler maintenance, and might well have no real knowledge of a problem or lack of it in logistics.

Getting a better balance in our view of manufacturing and the supply chain means the quality of software combined with the skill of people and their ability to share information that is properly tied to the realities of retailing, manufacturing, and the supply chain. That is, a move to more sharing and more quality of sharing.

SUMMING UP: SUPPLY CHAIN MODELING

Any model of the supply chain today has to embrace the advantages of the new and ever-changing technology that applies. This can range anywhere from communication systems for truck drivers to servers that coordinate with vast data warehouses filled with the incredible wealth of data on compliance, tracking, and order entry. There is no way to go back to paper models or linear models. Any new model will have to successfully deal with all the nuances of a customer of one within the context of different cultures, education level, aesthetic awareness, and means.

Chapter

18

MAKING IT RIGHT: A GLOBAL PERSPECTIVE

There is no way the world will survive in the long run with a few favored suppliers and supplied peoples, while there are many unsupplied and needy. It is not even good business.

The challenges in creating an effective and sustainable supply chain will be the struggles for affordable fuel, including wood and coal, and its transportation; potable water from existing sources or from regular and reliable distribution centers; adequate agricultural supply; clean air; necessary transportation facilities; a craft to manufacturing capability; and health care and its availability. Many of these needs are in conflict with each other, and businesses are in conflict as to who can get what and for how much.

All of these needs require having a responsive supply chain in place and the logistics to manage the details. The damaged and incomplete infrastructure of the United States and of many other parts of the world (e.g., Africa, India) will eventually be unable to sustain business—or our societies. The world cannot last half-supplied and half-unsupplied.

MAKING IT RIGHT IS NOT EASY

To a man with a hammer, all things look like a nail. To an observant person, nuance of difference is what the world is all about. To supply someone often is to make them dependent as is the United States on foreign oil, China on U.S. waste paper, and the world more and more on Chinese steel making and other manufacturing. Balance within the world's supply chain is necessary, as is an increased understanding of the relationships between events and processes, which may be more important than the events or processes themselves.

In the supply chain, the relationship between a ship and its speed, customs and its pace, or the dock and its availability is a calculation, and can be critical in just-in-time delivery. The same is true on the humble level of truck delivery. A well-organized fleet of trucks can fulfill faster and better than many trucks acting singly. In a fleet, the truck nearest to a demand can be dispatched to fulfill that demand, rather than having a single truck far away try to do the same thing.

WEARABLES

A wearable computer is, more or less, a computer that can be worn by a human being with full PC functions, including a keyboard, flat screen, and power source—not some $199 PDA. Once again the idea of a wearable computer is not new; Ed Thorp and Claude Shannon of MIT invented it in 1961 to predict roulette wheel motion. Five years later, Evan Sutherland at MIT created the first computer-based head-mounted display. Not to be outdone, Douglas Engelbart at SRI invented the first one-hand keyboard system in 1968. The system included online processing, word processing, split windows, hypermedia, a mouse, and desktop conferencing.

There are already companies offering wearable computers. Xybernaut's Mobile Assistant is a wearable that uses a head-mounted display, sports a Pentium MMX CPU, and has voice recognition and activation. Xybernaut sees its applications in clean rooms, warehousing, and repair work. It is able to access files, send email, and connect with the Internet. Clearly, the technology of the individual units is well along. It may be that the hardest part will be scale of function, cost, weight, and sustained power.

What, we might ask, will be the eventual effects of wearable computers in the enterprise, in the warehouse, in the factory? Will we plug in, or will we use a radio frequency device to communicate? The latest mobile technology from Symbol Technologies is offering a wearable computer and scanner to be used in picking and sorting in a warehouse or distribution center. Will we therefore take on a wearable that connects to our manufacturing, warehouse, logistics, planning role, or our function? Will some wearable computers be capable of multiple roles and functions?

The new technology will continue to support adaptive behavior of mechanisms and devices. The direction of new technology such as sensors, RFID, and robotics is to create a responsive world, whether we like it or not. It is the direction our technology is going. People with wearable technology will be working with tools that are themselves self-acting or knowledgeable to a degree. They will work within an adaptive network to coordinate the supply chain process on many levels, for many clients, and to the final end of fulfilling the demand of one customer.

SYNCHRONIZING WORLD TRADE BY SUPPLY NETWORKS

At the present moment, the thought of synchronizing world trade may seem ridiculous, but it is not. If companies, manufacturers, shippers, and retailers have a handle on their supply chains, then the substructure of a world supply chain has building blocks that will, in time, be made available. This may call for a big fight, as many companies will argue that their supply chains are of a proprietary nature, and are the basis for their business advantage. There are ways to overcome this: As a cooperative world supply chain group grows, the cost of staying out would become prohibitive. There would be a point at which the benefits of participating in such a cooperative would outweigh the disadvantages.

Sarbanes-Oxley can be looked at as a burden and a heavy cost. Sarbanes-Oxley is a hefty and costly set of U.S. government rules that requires companies to keep track of business accounting transactions in detail. A minority of companies is making use of the process and data related to the process to gain a business advantage. The information needed to manage a global supply chain is to a great extent, at least on the financial side, the same information needed to comply with Sarbanes-Oxley. This congruence, along with increased global trade, has augmented the interest in and use of global trade management (GTM) software, and may be a clarion call for more broadly based supply chain integration on a world basis. GTM gives a company a set of software applications that help account for and expedite customs, logistics requirements, language and currency translation, orders, bills of lading, and other global documents involving exchange rates, tolls, and security requirements.

GLOBALIZATION AND RISK

The company treasurer is now more and more a part of the efficient management of a supply chain. The flow of goods must be matched in visibility with the flow of money. At the highest level, achieving compliance with Sarbanes-Oxley depends on having timely, accurate, and complete information. It calls for establishing process controls, and these are the same success factors required to create a more secure and efficient global trade. Sarbanes-Oxley forces companies to examine their processes and controls, which should ultimately lead to actions that result in simpler, more efficient, and better controlled supply chain and logistics processes—and, in the process, may also improve financial performance.

Globalization adds complexity and risks to supply chain processes, which corporate executives must take into account when analyzing their operations and addressing investors. As supply chains become more fragmented and dispersed, the risk for terrorism, theft, smuggling, counterfeiting, and other issues also increases. An across-the-border shipment may change hands many times. It involves completing and filing dozens of documents and interfacing with different parties. There are hundreds of regulations and trade agreements that change constantly. With regard to establishing controls, the global trade process is probably one of the most critical areas that corporate executives must have on their radar screens.

Companies that trade globally face an increased level of financial risk. There are custom duties, taxes, transportation charges, and currency exchange rates; but there are other hidden factors that also influence profit, such as the cost of increased inventory. The further problem of longer cash-to-cash cycles due to customs clearance delays and security is a major issue in this arena. Several initiatives such as Smart and Secure Trade Lanes and Operation Safe Commerce have conducted pilot tests to identify vulnerability points along supply chains and to evaluate how technology such as RFID can increase both visibility and security, helping to lower the level of risk that companies face when they do business in the global marketplace.

There are certainly numerous other costs associated with Sarbanes-Oxley compliance, especially for small companies. Justifying these costs is difficult if companies view the effort simply as an exercise in complying. But if companies view Sarbanes-Oxley as an opportunity to create a smoother supply chain process, then the business case is much clearer, and the benefits in the long term will be much greater.

IMPROVING PLACES

So let's leave finances and Sarbanes-Oxley and proceed. Cities should be conceptualized as transportation and distribution centers, and not merely as architectural, tourist, or residential objects. As they are designed today, cities are rotten transportation and distribution centers. Access has been often the last thing considered in block and building design. Rails have moved people around the city, but have moved goods only in limited ways. Subway tracks, for instance, have never been used to move goods, even though they are used for transportation only minimally during late-night and early morning hours.

The city is a reflection of city design from a thousand or more years ago, and those parameters no longer work for us today. A city has to operate on many physical levels. If a city is to work, it should have transportation levels: one for people and one for goods, or a system that can be intermodal. The cost, of course, would be prohibitive. If we take an existing Wal-Mart distribution center and think of it as the base for a small city, we would be getting closer to today's living and working needs.

Until the 1920s, many towns and cities were linked by interurban railways. These were destroyed methodically by the automotive companies and replaced by buses. But today's buses do not have a right of way, and the interurban railways did to an extent. They had one great drawback: level grade crossings of streets. We need regional rail systems that can go by rail directly to large distribution centers, and far fewer trucks within city environs.

The regions of most nations should be connected by a combination of rail, truck, and air rather than an interstate highway system. Rail and road, terminal and hub all need to be designed in concert. Therefore, developing nations should not use the United States or Europe as a model—most particularly not the U.S. model.

As with nations, the world needs a transportation and distribution plan. The existing structure is not even demand driven. Where there is no real transportation and distribution system, there is no real demand economy. The big challenge in building a global economy is not the amount of information but the political cooperation, the corporate cooperation, and the availability of infrastructure.

SUMMING UP: A WORLD SYNCHRONIZED

Getting the world synchronized and adopting an organically operative and adaptive supply chain for the planet is no simple task. Regulations such as Sarbanes-Oxley help to standardize the documentation of transfers and financial processes, and that is probably where we must start.

The connectivity of people, as with cell phones and, eventually, wearable computers, makes it possible to get started. We can eventually migrate from knowing where our children are or how our stocks are doing to knowing how the supply chain is working for me, for you, and for us. If you want to make the world right, find a simple thing to improve, or find a way to do without it and prosper.

Chapter 19

AN ATLAS ACT: REPAIRING THE GLOBAL SUPPLY CHAIN

Fixing the world's supply chain and logistics, or even that of the United States, is no easy proposition; it is fraught with political issues, landmines, and levels of red tape and mismanagement in too many sectors, particularly in high places.

However, if corporations and entrepreneurs are going to grow their businesses through reaching more customers one at a time, fixing the world's supply chain and the infrastructure that supports the supply chain is a high priority. The world is out of balance logistically, badly out of balance. Unfortunately, beyond the cost, which will be staggering, progress can also be held back by government delays and by proprietary interests on the part of corporations, trade blocs, and associations. Nevertheless, the cost to not fix the world's supply chain will be more than staggering at both ends: the business end that supplies and the consumer end that receives.

When the United States outsources, one nation receives the business of manufacturing, for instance, but also suffers the consequences of manufacturing due to an inadequate governmental control of and interest in the environment. China manufactures for the West and pollutes itself. The West receives the profits but China becomes the industrial power. Who wins?

IMPROVING THE INFRASTRUCTURE

The long-range implications are a product of things already happening. The state of China's water and air, for example, is reaching a crisis point. On the one hand, the country improves its trade infrastructure; on the other, it jeopardizes its population's health and future viability.

The loss is not evenly distributed globally: The poor will inevitably suffer the most. The business and profit today goes to people in rich countries who can, for the most part, exist without the subsidies. The poor will have to be subsidized or they will cease to exist.

It's a national issue and it is an international issue. It has been a national issue for the United States since the founding of the country, and today it is a vital and critical issue. The United States has lost sight of a national vision of manufacturing through neglect and outsourcing, and of commerce through federal negligence in roads, rails, and air. China and, to a degree, India, appear to have a national vision. The world in general, though, has no vision at all.

INNOVATING TOMORROW

Innovation must become a shared world activity. Part of the innovation is to determine the priorities worldwide. Who needs what and what is possible? Once a situation becomes critical, triage will have to be applied and that means saving what can be saved and letting go what cannot be saved. If the most important problems are fixed now, and not later, then we may be able to stave off triage.

TRUCKING IN THE REARVIEW MIRROR

There are, as I have said, 2.7 million tractor trailer trucks on U.S. roads, using 51.4 billion gallons of fuel each year. It would behoove us to find many more ways to conserve. Fuel use in trucking has to be looked at innovatively. There are at least five major and interrelated factors: (1) drivers idle where they need not; (2) with education, drivers could operate their vehicles in a more fuel-efficient manner; (3) the truck's engine is being improved in efficiency as a response to regulation; (4) further energy-saving improvements are also being made by enlightened manufacturers such as Volvo; and (5) huge savings can be exacted by fleet or truck route management and delivery control with better and more widely distributed telematics.

Each of these factors is affected by the others. If a driver senses that delivery on time is more important than fuel, then he or she will be less conscious of conserving fuel. If the driver idles while having a sandwich, rather than turning off the engine, the cost of the meal is increased. When there are too many vehicles on the road, efficiency is reduced. In California, traffic is already being divided into "shifts" to relieve congestion. This is already helping the roads around Long Beach and Los Angeles ports. A further shift to more efficient intermodal transport would further help this condition in the ports. Goods should travel only by the mode that is most efficient. On an international level, all the above should be considered, and in addition, long-term leasing of equipment might be available at lower rates for developing nations.

The infrastructure needs maintenance and improvement on all its functional fronts:

- Ports are not just ports. A port is as good as its ability to cope with its road and rail traffic, in addition to handling, loading, and unloading ships. The port's infrastructure—including terminals, piers, open storage, garages, office road system, and rail, as well as the sea access—is the port.

- Rails are not just engines, flatbed cars, and boxcars chugging along rails. In fact, they are effective as a supply chain means to the degree that they have gone digital and gone intermodal. The exceptions are hauling long-distance products such as gravel, coal, and chemicals.
- Roads, like ports and rails, are not merely paved roadways. They are ramps, tolls, bridges, culverts, shoulders, gas and food facilities, signage, governance (financial and law enforcement), repair, and maintenance. Roads can be efficiently or inefficiently routed. Part of fixing roads is prioritizing roads: night traffic, priority lanes, and entrance pacing all help to improve the flow of traffic.
- To improve airways you need acreage, acreage, acreage! You can't build runways without acreage. You can't build new or improved airports without an extensive infrastructure that can reach out for tens of miles in a radial octopus of roads and facilities. Questions such as to hub or not to hub must be answered to solve part of the problem.

Of course, these elements of the transportation infrastructure all have to be brought together for unified planning and execution. There will be new challenges in their innovation as new technology emerges. Global digital communications, collaborative economies, and adaptive enterprises must all work in concert.

The advancement tomorrow of process will depend on the combination of already known technologies with strategies and elements that are unknown. The coordination of trade produces challenges on many levels, producing endless battles between the haves and the have-nots. Developing real free trade on a global level means free with all nations, and not just those that are economically preferred, such as World Trade Organization members or the usual European countries and the United States. Eventually, it needs to mean innovation in trade communications, such as low-cost hookups that are easily integrated without some kind of black box additive. That could translate into low-cost groups of servers and pollution-free connection to clean power.

INTEGRATING TOMORROW

To integrate information from a large array of world sources, we will need business intelligence dashboard access at all work levels. The dangers of today's dashboards are they can give a gloss—a distorted image of reality—as they only report what they receive, and what they receive can be tampered with, skewed by computer error, or misapplied, as in using the wrong algorithm. The old saying is junk in, junk out! These digital systems need to be balanced between automated and human alert management. Some data can be stored automatically, while other data needs human judgment and attention for complex and possibly intuitive issues. Issues involving human resources often require judgment by a person. Considerations of design, as in a computer-aided design process, require constant monitoring by a trained and sensitive human. Engineering decisions that apply to design for manufacture may be more a union/management consideration than a technical consideration.

There is no way we can stop the clock and expect to go back to a world where the measure of the competition was the shop across the street. Global trade is a reality. Our world now runs, for better or worse, on a global trade basis.

CAN GLOBALISM BE DESTRUCTIVE?

World interests and national interests are not congruent and often are at odds with one another. That which benefits one nation's trade may harm another's trade. The harm may be the erosion of the manufacturing base, as has been seen in the United States. This erosion is not merely a shift to cheaper suppliers, although in many cases it has stemmed from that. It is, as well, the decline of communities that once were sustained by their manufacturing bases, and that now experience loss of jobs and all the benefits that accompany having jobs. Specifically, this can mean seeing many older industrial cities such as Flint, Michigan, Gary, Indiana, and Paterson, New Jersey, rot, stagnate or die.

This decline may not be the direct result of foreign outsourcing. Other forces have been at work. For instance, Paterson's once-famed silk producing industry died as a consequence of many forces, including a change in the market demand. Other declines have been the result of leapfrog technology by foreign competitors, as was true of the U.S. steel industry in the 1960s and 1970s.

Regardless of the forces behind the decline, however, the results are most often an economic downturn or economic chaos for those individuals who do not have the means for a creative economic response—change of job or industry, change of location, change of mind-set, or change of lifestyle.

NEW INSOURCING

The word *insourcing*, as it is now generally being used, refers to foreign companies setting up businesses in the United States. This may benefit both the foreign nation and the U.S. worker and his or her community. It can help a local or state tax base. It can provide needed jobs, but the profits for the most part leave the country.

It is surely not a means of reinvigorating a national manufacturing effort. It is dependent manufacturing; the intellectual capital is owned by foreign concerns, and a good deal, or all profits, follow. Workers in South Carolina may build BMWs, but Germans and BMW own the ideas, the system, and the possibly substantial profits.

We need to see insourcing in a different light. It can be a means toward rejuvenating our industrial base. We can rebuild some of these devastated communities as manufacturing centers or support for manufacturing. We can identify market needs and with minimal financial shoring rebuild industries in those areas so badly brought down in the last 30 years. We can collaborate between national, state, and local authority and be forged together along with private interests if we care to and provide the energy. The United States can, as a nation, act as a unified business (we did it in World War II) for the greater good of the nation and its citizens. The interests of the less than powerful must be of consequence.

INFRASTRUCTURE REHAB

We need an infrastructure rehabilitation model that can travel. It should be flexible in its scale, range, cost, and complexity. It should give models with specifications for rail, road, sea, and air construction and their integration. It should be available over the Internet with supervisory help at a subsidized rate.

Large infrastructures such as the U.S. highway system develop their own inertia once they have been put in place. They are hard to remove, hard to convert, and hard to add to intelligently. We might start at the other end and try the core products and utilities; for instance, we might redesign or redo containers. They are about 50 years old in their design, which is a long period between models. A 53-foot container is too long for unloading and loading. It is like working in a long tube, and makes for an inefficient work process. It easy to pull by train or truck and stack on ships, but it is hard to use.

A redesign is in order, though there will be many naysayers who will say don't fix what isn't broken. The container probably needs to be a modular and flexible, Lego-like, set of sensing cubes that are plug-compatible in different configurations depending on load and carrier and control system.

Or we might start on a different set of infrastructures, such as the information infrastructure and server systems and their support and communications. Servers and their distribution have not reached a final stage. They are vital in helping to bring the information flow together with the physical flow of materials, components, and products. Having them right is a task of the highest order. Failure to do so jeopardizes both information and physical processes and business generally along with business profit.

TIPS AND TRENDS FOR ADAPTIVE BUSINESS

Several paramount trends have initiated the need for business change that is both closely timed and adaptive. These trends are:

- **Digitize it!** The challenge is conversion to global digital communication methods that are wireless, portable, powerful, and run nearly everything. This leads to an economy of ideas, relationships, and useful information as opposed to one that focuses on things, centralization, and the status quo.
- **Partner it!** The changing collaborative economy that is beyond political borders and simple corporate interest, and now moves toward the adaptive enterprise, is most available to those who choose partners, and wisely.
- **See it!** The need in business is for real-time visibility of process in order to make distributed control and decision making strategically competitive. We will have to make nanometer-sized objects and processes visible as well. We must see it clearly within the exabytes of information flowing at us.
- **Synch it!** The creation of synchronized business processes to allow for well-coordinated response to business and customer demand is a necessity.
- **Tech it!** Opportunities will emerge from new technologies such as identification technology, sensor technology, and advanced mobile robotics and communication. They need to be applied intelligently, wisely, and discreetly to ensure the security of personal data.
- **Level it!** Modern organizations are best organized with people working on basically the same level as teams, and not in a pyramid fashion with the boss at the apex.

- **Know it!** There is no good reason not to have all business processes visible to those who need to know.

SUMMING UP: AN ATLAS OVERVIEW

The correction on a global scale of both physical and information infrastructures will be essential for a supply chain that is sustainable in the long term. We need to integrate information, and thereby to produce the marching orders for getting the goods to people worldwide as needed, with a view to preserving the cultures and resources of people both developed and underdeveloped. If you want to help, you might start by finding out all the shortcomings of not transferring goods from one mode to the other. Why do we persist in doing things the expensive and polluting way?

Chapter 20

BY INTELLIGENT RESPONSE: THE FUTURE

Intelligent response is what a good supply network is all about. It is what we should expect from a well-oiled logistics effort. What it means is that those who would do business requiring a supply network and logistics execution should first and foremost offer an intelligent response to the demands of their customers, even just one. By intelligent response, we mean acting on information throughout the supply chain that is timely, accurate, and designed to give the customer the greatest benefit while offering the company a profitable transaction. The response depends on having information gathering, tracking, and recording at all points using the best technology such as bar codes, RFID, and sensors on materials, parts, assemblies, products, packages, transport means, in warehousing or sorting facilities, and throughout the sales and possible returns process. Intelligent response is response based on feedback from the whole supply chain or at least its pertinent parts.

FLUID PROCESSES GLOBALLY

Boundaries are becoming more fluid daily. Work now goes to where the workers are—often, these days, to China, India, and Mexico. In the future, almost all kinds of work will go where it is best suited. Product developments may no longer be in the country that is the origin of the idea (intellectual property). Packaging is done where it needs to be done; toys produced in China are most often packaged in China.

The biggest change is that collaboration occurs globally, making the location of any one product or process less important. The satellites that inform our work can be accessed from almost anywhere. We don't need telephone poles down the street or telegraph cables along the railroad track. Simple location is now a dated factor.

Shipping by air and by ship is a global business by ownership. The terminals are global; the ships are global. Containerization started in the United States, but is now a Chinese business: China manufactures 85 percent of the containers and is the largest user of them. China makes the most of them, fills the most of them, and ships the most of them for U.S. and world customers.

ROLES IN A FLUID PROCESS

There are specific roles within global trade. People all over the world are already, or learning to be, consumers for better or worse. Yesterday's supplier was across the street and now the supplier is across the ocean and on another continent. Manufacturers used to be in three regions: North America, Europe, and Japan. Now the shift is to Asia generally, with alternate operations developing in South America and Eastern Europe. Invention is beginning to take place globally. The international chain store has become the international supply chain store, and world entrepreneurs are being born everywhere and every day. Where there is an international consumer demand, whether personal, industrial, or governmental, there will be opportunity. Where there is opportunity, there will be demand. International monetary funding is fluid and electronic. Money follows the supply chain digitally, and what better way to reach one customer satisfactorily at a time?

It is well to remember that there are hundreds of millions of new consumers out there. China, India, and South America are on their way in terms of consumer growth, but Africa and much of Asia are untapped. It is hard to think of anyplace at which we couldn't manufacture, ship, and retail in this age if we cared to make it an objective. The world holds over six billion potential customers, of whom only a fraction are being reached today.

HUSBANDRY

The consequence of having all things in motion is a great increase in the volumes of communication, resulting in the opportunities to track, manage, and report on actions and events at a remote location.

When we use Google, for instance, we are farming information. We reap what we search, but the real measure of information reliability is cross-checking and adding in those factors not within Google. No researcher worth their salt stops at secondary and tertiary sources, and business managers shouldn't either. Getting close to the process means finding the roots of the process, and the roots are down in the dirt where they belong.

If a business manager uses business intelligence (BI) software, there has to be a degree of skepticism, a modicum of doubt. The automation may bring the information into one place and make it accessible, but we still have to judge as to what information is vital and what is trash. Our response has to be based on what we take in. Our response to events and changes is the basis for our survival.

Adaptive behavior is the world of today's commerce. Service in business is customer solution–centered. This is the way the present day supply chain works. It allows full visibility of shipments for the supplier and the customer, and it allows for changes to that shipment in seconds. It allows the owner of the shipment the capability to wrest financial advantage out of information in real time, and at the same time, satisfy the demand from one customer.

BEYOND AUTOMATING TO BUSINESS PARTNERING

Times are changing, and as FedEx, UPS, DHL, and other 3PLs move into the future, they will be doing less driving, less flying, and more thinking. Planning, coordination, and execution will supersede packaging, pick up, and delivery. These companies will continue to refine their material flow and their use of tools. Automating when it was first practiced acted on tools and machines. This was followed by automation becoming the engine of computing. Codes created algorithms that acted automatically on information. Now is the time when coordination and synchronization between tools and information is the key to growth and dominance in business. Real-time and adaptive control takes processes beyond automation. It is not enough for processes to be automatic. New sensors (e.g., proximity, temperature, pressure) and today's robotics are adaptation driven and not merely automatic. Their responses are not mechanical so much as being toward an organic response—made up of a set of compact adaptive responses that interact and re-respond as environment and conditions change.

In a similar way, business processes must be responsive and use the feedback of the moment as the means for action, the means for control adjustment. Processes have to be sensitive to human needs as well, which dooms a purely automated approach. We thus describe the world of today's commerce: It is a solution-centered business, and the solutions are for people. We now see the gradual deployment of new technology that will span from supplier to customer using wireless telecommunications as a means to receive information from those millions or billions of different automated sensors and human developed sources.

A SUPPLY NET TSUNAMI!

The practice of using synchronized commerce networks has already been taken up by IBM, Apple, Dell, Wal-Mart, Target Stores, Harley-Davidson, Toshiba, and others. Synchronized commerce is a direct extension of the pull theory of logistics and the supply net. It is an ideal expression of demand-driven business, and that means a customer-centric process. A synchronized commerce network establishes key commerce points (partnerships, collaborations, contracts with 3PLs and shippers, etc.) throughout the global supply network that act as with one voice, because they act out of one database and database management system. There are no serious loose ends, no incongruent sets of data, no unrecorded and uncontrolled activity off to the side.

SUPPLY CHAIN AS A SUSTAINABLE CONCEPT

The *supply chain* as a term is a misnomer today. It implies a linear arrangement in which one event leads or is linked to another event. The actual facts of supply are nonlinear, and the linkages are three dimensional, multiple, and in simultaneous time. The events of supply are cyclical, hopefully synchronous, and global. The Supply Chain Council's SCOR model underscores the linearity and can no longer be a useful paradigm. The linear model of a supply chain is not sustainable and to a great extent has already died.

Events in a real supply network (for want of a better word) act on each other and have a more organic than mechanical relationship. I believe an organically modeled supply chain is sustainable. That means that if you want to build the right supply chain and capture each customer and their loyalty, then make it organic. I see an image of a bio-supply system, an organically operated sourcing, and a biologically metered response. An organic system, unlike a mechanical system, has internal response built in. However, these responses in an organic system can be automatic (as with our digestion) or intentional (as with the decisions we make when driving a car, using both our hand-eye coordination and our mind). Mechanical systems may have feedback as in a ball governor on an engine, but it is simplistic and holds to its performance regardless of environmental changes. An organic system has feelers inside and outside and it is able to balance its actions upon understanding the interplay of both.

INSIGHTS BY SYNCHRONIZING

The synchronized supply chain is a series of supply chain solutions that cross all forms of transportation modes (air, land, and sea). It is a solution that combines sales, marketing, finance, and all forms of technology resources into one controllable and visible database.

Synchronized commerce operates in real time and gives an enormous advantage to customers of FedEx, DHL, and particularly UPS, because they know what is being shipped, from where to whom, and how. The process tells them when a specific package or load of goods will arrive where, and when it will reach its ultimate destination. Others in the industry, such as AMR Research, call this the demand-driven supply chain.

The synchronized supply chain (and the demand-driven one) works with intermodal exchanges between air and rail, air and truck, and truck and rail. A demand-driven supply chain can be a subset of a synchronized supply chain, as it in principle acts only to meet demand and is not necessarily geared to take in other factors, such as the nature and extent of a partnership or collaboration. The synchronized system operates within the many distribution centers that receive, sort, and distribute as needed products, bulk goods, packages, and mail. It allows for a variety of schedules in terms of delivery priority: same day, overnight, next day, and two day. Synchronization will make additional services seamless with those that now exist. Synchronization can be described briefly as:

1. Combining of orders by timing and mode
2. Coordination of multiple suppliers' products and delivery
3. Coordination of information processing as a flow with physical processing
4. Demand and capacity balance

To be synchronized is to be flexible in your response as demand changes from supplier, process, carrier, and customer.

COLLABORATIVE ECONOMIES AND ADAPTIVE ENTERPRISES

There are no monopolies on the control and understanding of change. The ability to change is as fluid and restless as mercury. The ability to change a business is viable only while operating the business in real time with partners. As Kevin Kelly has said, "If you are not in real time you're dead."

The new responsive and adaptive enterprise has to be organized around synchronized activity with active distributed control in order to capitalize on change, and not just simply modify incrementally existing business procedures.

SECOND GUESSES

Here are a series of cautionary words about various elements of logistics and supply chain planning.

- *Capacity planning.* The question has to once again be asked: Can you really plan capacity? You can try, but what happens in

a supply chain trauma such as Hurricane Katrina? What happens if the one thing needed for production is sitting in a ship off of the Louisiana coast and there is a port shutdown?
- *Real time.* It does not, in fact, exist and cannot, because it leaves no room for processing—what is meant is eliminating, as much as possible, the lag time between an event and our knowledge of the event.
- *Synchronization.* To be synchronized within a complex event or complex organization requires new levels of coordination. There must be openness in communication (sharing, comparing, adjusting simultaneously). There needs to be a physical or electronic network in place to receive the messages instantly and the response of the parties involved just as instantly. We are talking of a team rather than a crowd, an integrated group such as a dance company rather than onlookers. Synchronized teams or groups flock like geese rather than acting independently like eagles.

    "One river born from many streams/Roll in one blaze of blinding light." (from George William Russell's poem "Salutation," 1866)

    Note: the concept of synchronicity predates the supply chain and logistics industry and the UPS definition, as the work of Jung will testify in a general way and Joseph Jaworski, in his book *Synchronicity,* does in a more specific business way.
- *Just-in-time.* It is a goal that if fully realized could become its own worst enemy—no slack, no emergency, no stopgap. It is geared to a system that must not fail nor even hesitate. In principle, it is grand, but the pressure it exacts may have a price, particularly if more widely practiced.
- *Lean* or *agile.* Can we be too lean, too agile? Rendering out the fat is only the beginning. The process must entail zero defects and great design and engineering. Lean cannot be endlessly applied. There is just so much fat in any system, and some of it may have a purpose.

- *Reengineering.* Yes, get close to the process but do not throw the executives and workers out with the bath water. If the processes are wrong to begin with, what benefit is there in getting closer to the process? Reengineering is fundamentally the analysis and process of remake of the methods of business. It takes in who knows what, what is done, and what is the effect.
- *Airline hubs.* Commercial hubs make all kinds of sense as the nodes of the supply chain network as defined by an enterprise or a nation—even if they may not work so well for passengers.
- *RFID tracking.* It has been touted and praised. It has been questioned and vilified by some. Is it really better than sliced bread? Better and more reliable than bar codes? Will you bet the store, the warehouse, the business on it? How do we deal with the privacy issues?
- *On demand.* Will the age of demand give way to some other word? What is beyond demand? Will it be regulation or scarcity beyond fulfillment? There is no denying that demand will continue, but will the ability to supply that demand continue to grow, or are we in danger of a world gripped by scarcity and vital needs?

CHAIN MAIL

"Wherever possible, transmit the instructions to make a product, rather than transporting the actual product" is a rough translation of an IKEA proverb. Whenever possible, remove motion in products and transport. Replace gears with circuits, as we have with telephones, radios, and music players. Replace actual objects in transport with virtual objects (e.g., replace a set and actors in a theater with a film on a DVD). The movies and TV have given the masses the opportunity to experience, at least secondhand or on film (or DVD), what used to require physical staging. The same effect has happened in tracking of goods: Paper in endless streams and piles has been replaced by referable and easily storable digital information on databases.

NEW TOOLS, NEW WAYS

Managers need to be informed in a real-time world and should carry out the decision-making process and its subsequent operation in a real-time context. The advent of business intelligence dashboards has made this a possibility. There are difficulties: lack of data warehouses within an enterprise, lack of other centralized enterprise data, and a lack of reliability of the data. Real time with delays between communications is not real time at all. The two greatest faults associated with information are lack of quality and lack of sharing. Information such as the processing of goods needs to be just-in-time. This is just-in-time to the right people, with the right amount and quality of information, at the right time. This broadly based task is not easily accomplished.

GATHERING INNOVATING AND PROCESS ENHANCING

None of us can embrace all change. Intelligent response means getting innovation, process enhancing, and demand management together as a set of coordinated plans and in practice. It is easy to say and hard to do. However, UPS, Dell, and Wal-Mart each in their own arena have managed to do just this consistently.

The old way was through linear steps and by a process of push. The new way is by a process of pull. No action within the process of innovation is independent of the other actions. No action within an optimized process is independent of the other actions. No action within the process of demand management is independent of the other actions. The linkage within these three forces is critical and, in turn, the linkage between demand, enhancement, and innovation is critical. No action in any of the principal strategies can be independent of the other actions.

SUMMING UP: INTELLIGENT RESPONSE

We have examined the situation of our supply networks and logistics applications from donkeys to inlay tags, nano machines, and Internet-enabled perspectives. Any attempt to put off understanding, planning, and intelligent implementation will just aggravate the situation all the more. Our reaction to the supply chain has to be by intelligent response.

We are the motile tissue within the adaptively responsive and synchronized supply chain that is taking advantage of the world's electronic and strategic resources. We are the planners and the balancers and the farmers of Earth's rich crop of materials and potential products. We need our innovative talents, unfettered, to control and guide the tools of logistics and the systems of the supply network. Our best bet is an organic model that is capable of immediate and intelligent feedback and correction or enhancement. It is, of course, a vision; however, without a vision, our future is lost.

All the Earth's people are our neighbors, and they are all customers—or could be. Imagine what it would be like if we reached out to all of them at least as possible customers or employees and an extension of existing business. China is an example of the explosion of a middle class to whom all the world can trade. Developed nations need to help other nations and the world move toward intelligent and shared responses. This help can be not to just pending disasters but to the real day-to-day needs of people worldwide. We need to move away from a reactive response to need, toward an interactive and continuously intelligent response to need. It is better for us to call need "demand" and place needs in the supply and demand cycle. There is enough food and water; we just need a better means of getting them to customers—and making that supply chain profitable on a long-term basis to those who give and to those who receive.

Acknowledgments

I would like to acknowledge the help and encouragement by the following people and organizations: John Willing my stellar agent; Jim Martin the logistics expert; the staff of Kaplan Publishing including Jennifer Farthing; Shannon Berning; Karina Cueto; Siobhan McKiernan Flahive; the staff of *Managing Automation* magazine including David Brousell and Chris Chiappinelli; the staff of *Inbound Logisitics* including Felecia Stratton, editor, and Keith Biondo, publisher; AMR Research including its CEO Tony Friscia and staff Bruce Richardson, Kevin O'Marah, and Kevin Reilly; the stafff of ARC Advisory Group including its CEO Andy Chatha and Adrian Gonzalez, supply chain analyst; Michael Topolovac CEO of Arena; and from Forbes.com, business editor David Andelman, editor-in-chief Paul Maidment, and managing editor Dan Bigman; and Max Katz, writer and filmmaker for his listening patience.

I would also like to acknowledge the following companies and associations that have cooperated in my research and writing: UPS, FedEx, DHL, IBM, Wal-Mart, Steve & Barry's, IKEA, Teradata, Tradestone Software, American Trucking Association, Council for Supply Chain Management Professionals, and PHH First Fleet.

PERMISSIONS ACKNOWLEDGMENTS

Robert A. Malone and Kaplan Publishing would like to kindly acknowledge the publishers who provided permission to reprint from the following articles, which were written by the author and have been excerpted and adapted in *Chain Reaction*.

Reprinted by permission of Inbound Logistics © 2007 by Inbound Logistics:
"Talking Tactics with IBM," January 2005, *Inbound Logistics*.

Reprinted by permission of FORBES Asia Magazine © 2007 Forbes Media LLC:
"An Increasingly Big Deal," 8/4/06 Forbes Asia.

Reprinted by permission of FORBES.com © 2007 Forbes.com:
"I Can't See," 8/30/06 Forbes.com; "BAM to the Rescue," 10/25/05 Forbes.com; "Help Wanted, Truck Drivers," 5/4/06 Forbes.com; "Airfreight Grows Globally," 3/16/06 Forbes.com; "The Reverse Side of Logistics," 11/30/05 Forbes.com; "Supplying China," 10/2/06 Forbes.com; "A Logistical Look at China," 10/2/06 Forbes.com; "Where Cash Meets Trade," 5/19/06 Forbes.com.

Reprinted by permission of Thomas Publishing Company, LLC, © 2007 by Thomas Publishing LLC:
"Incremental Change," May 2004, *Managing Automation;* "Managing Risk in Business (The Age of Risk)," November 2006, *Managing Automation;* "Facing the Dysteleological," June 2002, *Managing Automation;* "Disruptive Technologies?," February 2005, *Managing Automation;* "Going the E-Way," July 2005, *Managing Automation;* "American Manufacturing," March 2005, *Managing Automation;* "Manufacturing Turns 200," July 2002, *Managing Automation;* "Sold for Less than Retail," April 2006, *Managing Automation;* "Another Look at Core Competency (Hollowing Out the Core)," August 2006, *Managing Automation;* "Beat to Quarters," March 2005, *Managing Automation;* "An Organic View, March 2004, *Managing Automation;* "Wearable Computers," November 2001, *Managing Automation;* "Insourcing to the Rescue," July 2006, *Managing Automation*.

Index

A

Aberdeen Group, 55
Acquisitions, 103
Adaptation, 19
Adaptive behavior, 35-36, 233-34
Adaptive business, 228-29, 237
Adaptive change, 54, 78
Adaptive model, 208-9
Agile, 238
Agile manufacturing, 139-40
Airports, 162, 187
Air transport
    airfreight forwarding, 93
    growth, 98
    history, 106-7
    hubs, 166-67, 239
    improvements, 224
    innovation, 46
Allen-Bradley pyramid model, 199
Allowable innovation, 19
Amazon.com, 75, 115, 145
American Messenger Company, 104
American Trucking Association
    industry employment, 99-100
    infrastructure improvement, 174
    innovation techniques, 43
    process context, 55
AMR Research, 192, 201
Anchorage Airport, 166-67
Anchorage Economic Development Council, 188-89
Answering services, 136
Anticipatory design, 26
Apple Computer, Inc., 8, 135-36
Apple Store, 147-48
ARC Advisory Group, 193
Arena Solutions, 191
ARPANET, 104
Artificial intelligence, 35, 80
Asian ports, x, 163
Asimov, Isaac, 48
Association of American Railroads, 172
Automation
    explanation of, 61-62
    future trends, 7-8, 234-35
    growth of, 61-69
    of information, 48, 123-24

B

Ballard, Robert, 31, 32
Bar code
    application, 42
    origins, 87
    patent, 92
    scanner, 145
    USPS and, 107
Baran, Paul, 74
Bayonne Bridge, xi
Bed Bath & Beyond, xii
Bell, Alexander Graham, 72, 73, 119
Berners-Lee, Tim, 74
Big box warehouse stores, 144
Bit, 4
Blasgen, Rick D., 190
BMW, 10
Boston Manufacturing Company, 118-19
Breakdowns, 34-35
Brookings Institution, 165
Bulk cargo inspection, 24
Business assisted management, 15, 67-68
Business intelligence, 15, 233
Business processes
    adaptive change, 54
    context, 55
    core incompetence, 57-58
    distributed control, 53-54
    enhancement, 51-52
    innovation, 47-48
    visibility, 55-56, 58
    waste removal, 56-57
Business start-ups, 12
Byte, 4

C

Calder, Alexander, 27
Canals, 161
Capacity planning, 237-38
Carmichael, Gil, 169
Cars, 10
Casey, George, 105
Casey, Jim, 42, 90, 104-5
Caterpillar, 193

245

Index

Cell phones, 11
Centralized control, 51
Champy, James, 52
Change
   adaptive behavior, 35-36
   in information flow, 54
   management, 17-20
China
   airfreight, 188
   environmental concerns, 194
   GDP, 188, 189
   logistics, 189-90
   manufacturing, 190-91
   pharmaceutical industry, 194
   ports, 188
   R&D, 190
   supply chain, 188-89, 195
   trash production, 192
Circuit switching technique, 74
Circus ramping, 89
Clarke, Arthur C., 74-75
Cognistics, Inc., 170
Coke, 194
Collaboration, 232
Collaborative economies, 237
Collaborative logistics, 170-71
Commercial carriers. See also DHL; FedEx; UPS
   challenges, 114
   customers, 114-15
   innovations, 46-47
Communication
   changes in, 4
   computers and, 73-74
   elements of, 72
   global, 71
   Internet, 74
   inventions, 72-73
   partnerships, 78-79
   revolution, 74
   RFID technology, 76-77
   satellite, 74-75
   wireless, 79
Complexity, 14-15
CompUSA, 145
Computer integrated manufacturing, 125, 199-200
Computer-to-computer networks, 73-74
Container ports, 163
Containerships
   need for, 46-47, 94
   size, 99, 164-65
Control, 51-59
Conveyors, 120
Core competency
   Dell, 140
   explanation of, 134
   IBM, 137
   retail, 147
Core incompetence, 57-58
COSCO, 165
COSMOS, 109
Costco, 153
Council of Supply Chain Management Professionals, 190
Cross docking, 47
CSX Intermodal, 172
Customers/consumers, 146

D

Darwin, Charles, 19
Data systems, 48
Data warehouse, 6, 64
da Vinci, Leonardo, 40
Decision making, 15
Deep sea ports, 164
Delivery service model, 44
Delivery system, 9
Dell
   core competencies, 140
   demand methodology, 126
   idea development, 135
   innovations, 45
   pull strategy, 123
   supply chain strategy, 139-40
Demand access, 73-74
Demand driven supply network, 201-2, 236
Demand management, 145-46
Demand methodology, 126
Deming, W. Edwards, 121, 198
Deming model, 198
Department of Defense, 14
Devol, George, 92
DHL
   acquisitions, 103
   air cargo hub, 167
   Asia-Pacific service area, 116
   competitive advantage, 103, 110
   customers, 115
   employment, 111

Index

history, 32, 106, 145
innovations, 108
international service, 108, 110
Internet and, 113
precursor of, 90
wireless communication, 78
Diebold, John, 48, 123-24
Diesel, Rudolf, 89
Digital, 32
Distributed control
computer-to-computer networks, 74
model, 53-54
origins, 51
Distributed manufacturing, 131-32
Distribution center, xii-xiii
function of, 176, 177-78
goods in/out, 176-77
Hershey Foods, 178
Home Depot, 178
placement of, 176
precursors of, 88-89
reverse logistics, 178-81
RFID and, 177
size of, 178
Steve & Barry's, 158
traffic zones and, 111
UPS, 105, 111
Wal-Mart, 152, 154

Drewry Shipping Consultants, 165
Drexler, K. Eric, 6
Dubai Ports World, 164
Duke University, 7
Dysteleology, 28-29

E

eBay, 75
Economies of scope, 134
Edgewater Technology, 67
Edison, Thomas, 41, 72, 119
Education, 133
Efficiency, 119
E Ink, 13
Eisenhower, Dwight D., 92
Electronic data interchange, 73
Electronic product code, 77
eMachineShop.com, 80
Email, 74
eManufacturing, 79, 80
eManufacturing, Inc., 81
Empties, xii, 32-33
Engelbart, Douglas, 214
Enterprise resource planning
computer-integrated manufacturing, 200
explanation, 125
logistics management, 66
supply chain, 53, 95
Web-based solutions, 171

EPCGlobal, 77
eWorkcells, 80-81
Exabyte, 4-5
Expert systems, 35
Exports, xii, xiii

F

Federal-Aid Highway Act, 92
Federal Express Corporation. See FedEx
FedEx
acquisitions, 103
air cargo hub, 166-67
airfreight, 93, 107, 122
Asia-Pacific service area, 116
cargo growth, 98
competitive advantage, 103, 110
customers, 115
demand methodology, 126
employment, 111
history, 32, 106, 109-10, 145
innovations, 42, 109-10, 112
Internet and, 113
Kinko's Office and Print Services, 112
partnerships, 79
precursor of, 90
wireless communication, 78
Feedback, 123
FEMA, 23
Flexibility, 206-7
Flynn, Stephen E., 21-22

247

Index

Ford, Henry, 90, 119, 128
Ford Motor Company, 10, 90
Franchise, 24-25
Franklin National Bank, 144
Fresh Direct, 44
Friedman, Thomas, 12
Fuller, Buckminster, 26

G

Gates, Bill, 186
Gerald Desmond Bridge, 99
Gigabyte, 5
Global airfreight, 98
Global information, 5
Globalism, 12
Globalization, 216-17, 232-33
Global trade management, 68, 216
Gonzalez, Adrian, 193, 194, 195
Google, 6, 75, 76, 233
Greenspan, Alan, 19
Gross domestic product, xii
Ground transport, 99-100

H

Hammer, Michael, 52
Harrison, John, 86
Hershey Foods, 178
Hewlett-Packard, 136-37
Highway
　improvements, 224
　infrastructure, 93
　origins, 87-88

system, 186-87
trucking, 92
Hillman, Mark, 192
Hiratsuka, Yuichi, 7
Home Depot, xii, 178
Honeybee Robotics, 58
Hong Kong Airport, 166
Howland Hook, xi-xii
Husbandry, 233-34
Hutchinson Port Holdings, 164

I

IBM
　computer forecasts, 185-86
　core competencies, 137
　demand methodology, 126
　idea development, 135
　partnerships, 79
　procurement management, 138
　strategic advantage, 126
　supply chain strategy, 137-38, 203-5
IKEA
　demand methodology, 126
　growth, 157
　history, 156
　innovations, 94
　proverb, 239
　supply chain, 46, 147, 156, 157
Imports, xii-xiii
Industrial revolution, 88

Information
　adaptive network, 210
　automation, 124
　change, 54
　database, 125
　data volume, 5-6
　global, 5
　integration, 225
　magnetic media, 5
　processing of, 77
　quantities of, 4-6
　scales of, 4-5
　software, 64
　volume of, 63-64
Informix, 6
Infrastructure improvements, 222-24
Infrastructure rehabilitation model, 227-28
Innovation
　business processes, 47-48
　commercial carriers, 46-47
　global supply chain, 222
　imagination and, 42
　inventions, 40-41
　in manufacturing, 45-46
　observation-based, 40
　questions of, 39-40
　retail distribution, 47
　short cuts, 48
　steps, 44-45
　techniques for, 43-44
　trends, 49
Insourcing, 226-27
Insurance, 24-25

Index

Intel supply chain model, 207-8
Intelligent response, 231-41
Interchangeability, 18
Interchangeable parts, 118
Intermodal transportation
 air cargo hubs, 166-67
 beginnings, 93
 rail, 167-69, 187-88
 ships, 161-66
 system, 22
 Web-based solutions, 171
Intermodal Transportation Institute, 169
International Air Transport Association, 98
Internet
 business communication and, 74, 75
 power of, 79
 servers, 76
 supply chain, 75-76
 tracking systems, 113
 use, 11
iPod, 8

J

Jidoka, 124
Jung, Carl, 40
Just-in-time
 caution, 238
 delivery, 47
 strategies, 23
 Toyota Production System, 42, 124

K

Kamprad, Ingvar, 156
Kelly, Kevin, 237
Kepler, Johannes, 41
KFC, 194
Kilobyte, 5
Kinko's, 79, 112, 115
Kleinrock, Leonard, 73
Kmart, 144
Koulopoulos, Tom, 133-34
Kroger, 144

L

LAN Cargo, 167
Lean, 238
Lean manufacturing, 139-40
Lift and shift outsourcing, 134
Linear model, 235
Locks, 162
Logistic Collaboration Solutions, 170-71
Logistics
 business activity management, 67-68
 China, 189-90
 collaborative, 170-71
 coordination of, 127
 demand methodology, 126
 highway system, 93
 implications for, 13
 intermodal transportation, 169-70
 management software, 66
 origins, 88, 121
 paper consumption, 13-14
 pull theory, 235
 risk management, 25
 shipping container, 21
 stress-driven changes, 196
 supply chain and, 95
 timed, 89
 war application, 89-91
Logistics Group, 67
Los Angeles International Airport, 167
Louisville Airport, 167

M

Made-to-order, 45
Made-to-stock, 45
Maersk Line, 79, 164
Magnetic media, 5
Mail Boxes Etc., 79, 112
Mall of America, 145
Maltby, Donald, 179
Management control relationship, 199
Manufacturing
 accountable innovation, 19
 American system, 118-19
 changes in, 18-19
 demand driven, 128-29
 distributed model, 131-32
 evolution of, 117-29
 innovations, 45-46, 119-20

mass production, 120-21
pull methodology in, 122-24, 127-28
push strategy in, 120-21
roles, 134-36
silos, 125
Toyota Production System, 124
Manufacturing resource planning
computer-integrated manufacturing, 199-200
explanation, 125
supply chain, 53, 95
Marconi, Guglielmo, 73
Mars Rover, 58
Martin, Jim, 168
Mass production, 91
McCabe's Motorcycle Messengers, 105
McDonald's, 9
McLean, Malcolm, ix, 94
Meat packing industry, 119-20
Mechanical advantage, 87
Mechanical progress, 119
Mediterranean Shipping, 165
Megabyte, 5
Memphis International Airport, 109, 166
Merchants Parcel Delivery, 105
Miami International Airport, 167
Miniaturization, 6-8

Mobility, 133
Morse, Samuel, 72
Multitier supply chain processes, 55

N

Nanometer, 6
Nanotechnology, 6-8
National Nanotechnology Infrastructure Network, 6-7
Netezza, 6
Networks, 14-15
Nike, 194
Nistevo Corporation, 171

O

Off-shoring, 132
Olsen, Ken, 32, 186
On-demand, 239
On-demand software, 75-76
On-demand supply chains, 73, 74
One-off manufacturing, 42
Operator-centric manufacturing, 54
Oracle, 6, 12
Organization for Economic Co-operation & Development, 190
Outsourcing
answering services, 132
concerns, 202-3
origins, 24, 85
publishing, 132
retail, 151

P

Panama Canal, xi, 162, 195
Paper consumption, 13-14
Performance tracking methods, 55
Personal computers, 11
Petabyte, 5
Pharmaceutical industry, 194
Piggyback service, 168
Pizza Hut, 194
Poe, Bob, 188-89
Population, 10-11
Port
characteristics, 161
container inspections, 165
containerships and, 164-65
expenditures for, 162-63
growth, 163
infrastructure, 223
operators, 163-64
security issues, 163
Port (of)
Busan, 163
Hong Kong, 163
Long Beach, x
Los Angeles, x, xi, 99
New York/New Jersey, ix-xii
Rotterdam, 28
Seattle, 25
Shanghai, 162, 163
Shenzhen, 163
Singapore, 163, 164
Porter, Michael, 198

Index

Power distribution, 18-19
Principles of Scientific Management, The, 119
Process stability, 124
Procter & Gamble, 79
Procurement management, 138
Product lifecycle management, 65, 202
Products on-demand, 80-81
ProLogis, 189
PSA International, 164
Public Law 95-163, 109
Publishing industry, 136
Pull economy, 51-52
Pull manufacturing, 93
Pull methodology, 122-24, 127-28
Push economy, 51-52
Push manufacturing, 92
Push strategy, 120-21

Q-R

Quality control, 52, 94
Radio, 73
Radio frequency identification data
　compliance, 5
　DoD, 14
　Intel's use, 207-8
　by satellite, 76-77
　tagging, 47
　tracking, 112-13, 239
　Wal-Mart and, 14, 153-54
Rail transport
　carriers, 47
　competitive advantage, 100-101
　improvements, 224
　intermodal transportation, 167-69, 187-88
　productivity gains, 172-73
　technology, 172
RAND, 157
Reality
　consequences, 36
　misunderstanding, 32
　of process, 34-35
　response, 35-36
　technology and, 37-38
　traceable facts, 32-33
　understanding, 31-32
Real time, 238
Recycling, 36
　Red Hook, xi-xii
Redundancy, 56, 58
Reengineering, 239
Reengineering the Corporation, 52
Registration, Evaluation, Authorization and Restriction of Chemicals, 102
Remanufacturing, 114, 194
Retail
　adaptive system, 209-10
　chain stores, 144
　core competencies, 147
　credit cards and, 144-45
　customers/consumers, 146
　demand management, 145-46
　dependencies, 151-52
　distribution, 47
　evolution of, 143-59
　outsourcing, 151
　specialization, 148
　supply chain, 146-47, 149-59
　unified buying process, 149-50
Retail Forward, Inc., 155-56
Returns management, 114
Reverse engineering, 32-33, 43-44
Reverse logistics, 178-81
Richardson, Bruce, 201-2
Ringling Brothers and Barnum & Bailey Circus, 89
Risk management
　anticipation, 26
　big picture and, 27
　change and, 17-20
　flexibility, 26-27
　forecasting risk, 22-23
　globalization and, 216-17
　insurance, 24-25
　outsourcing and, 24
　plan execution, 23
　priorities, 23-24
　proactive, 28-29
　shipping container inspection, 20-21
　vulnerability, 21-22
Road system, 91-92

Index

Roberts, Lawrence, 113
Robotics, 48
Rule of negation, 91

S

Sam's Club, 152-53
Sarbanes-Oxley, 216, 217
SAS, 6
Satellite communication, 74-75
  RFID technology, 76-77
Schuebler, Jacob, 156
Sears, 145
Sea transport, 98-99
Sectional processing, 120
Security and Accountability for Every Port Act, 22
SEKO, 102
Seoul Incheon Airport, 167
Service-oriented architecture, 66, 68
7-Eleven, 144
Shannon, Claude, 72, 214
Shipping container
  inspection, 20-21, 24, 165
  supply and demand, 165-66
  vulnerability, 21-22
Shopping center, 144
Silos, 125
Size, 12-13
Smartsourcing, 133-34
Smith, Adam, 117
Smith, Gary, 204
Software
  business activity management, 67-68
  history, 63-64
  information management, 64
  invention of, 62
  on-demand, 75-76
  service-oriented applications, 68
  system management, 65-66
Starbucks, 9
Starkowsky, Joan, 179-80
Steinmetz, Charles, 41, 72
Steve & Barry's
  auto-replenishment system, 158, 159
  distribution centers, 158
  growth, 157
  licensing agreements, 158
Store-to-home delivery, 104-5
Suez Canal, 162
Sugarman, Gary, 157
Sun Microsystems supply chain, 136
Supply chain
  adaptive model, 208-10
  Big Mac, 9
  DoD, 14
  explanation of, 94-95
  flexibility, 206-7
  global perspective, 213-19
  history of, 85-95
  implications for, 13
  infrastrucutre and, 86
  Internet-enabled, 125
  iPod, 8
  J-I-T strategies, 23
  linear model, 235
  logistics and, 95
  management, 126
  McDonald's, 9
  origin, 121, 135
  reduction, 36-37
  rule of negation, 91
  strategic advantage of, 126-27, 128
  sustainable, 235-36
  vulnerability, 23
  Wal-Mart, 23
Supply Chain Council, 52-53, 235
Supply-chain operations reference, 53
Sutherland, Evan, 214
Symbol Technologies, 215
Synchronization, 215-16, 219, 235-38

T

Tacoma Bridge, 33
Target, 144
Taylor, Frederick W., 119
Technology, 3, 37-38, 88-89
Telegraph, 72-73
Telephone, 73, 74, 119
Terabyte, 5, 6
Teradata, 6
Texas Transportation Institute, 100

Index

Third-party logistics providers (3PL)
  collaboration, 170-71
  computer-related applications, 101-2
  example of, 102-3
  growth of, 103
  partnerships, 79
  risk, 25
  role of, 101, 102
  wireless communication, 78
Thorp, Ed, 214
Tokyo Narita, 166
Tokyo University, 7
Tomlinson, Ray, 74
Topolovac, Michael, 191
Toyota, 42
Toyota Production System, 92, 124
Tracking
  commercial carriers and, 112
  Internet and, 113
  performance methods, 55
  RFID and, 34, 112-13
  system, 42
Trade imbalance, xii
TradeStone Software, 149-50
Transport system, 209
Transportation management software, 66
Triage, 23-24
Truck transport
  communication, 10
  highway system, 92
  innovations, 46-47, 223

trucking companies, 173-74
Turing, Alan, 41

U

United Air Express, 106
United Parcel Service. See UPS
United States Postal Service. See USPS
University of California (Berkeley), 5, 6
University of California (Los Angeles), 7
University of Wisconsin (Madison), 6
UPS
  acquisitions, 103
  air cargo hub, 166-67
  airfreight, 93, 106-7, 122
  Asia-Pacific service area, 115-16
  automation, 32
  beginnings, 90
  cargo growth, 98
  competitive advantage, 103, 110
  customers, 114-15
  delivery fleet, 111
  delivery volume, 111
  demand methodology, 126
  distribution centers, 105, 111
  employment, 111
  express service, 106
  golden link, 108-9
  history, 104-6, 107

innovations, 42, 112
international service, 110-11
Internet and, 113
partnerships, 79
precursor of, 90
pull strategy, 123
revenues, 111
strategic advantage, 126-27
tracking, 114
wireless communication, 78
U-shaped workspace, 42
USPS
  air cargo hub, 166-67
  automation, 32
  employment, 111
  innovation, 42

V

Value added networks, 77
Value chain, 198-99
Verrazano-Narrows, xi
Virtual operational data store, 77
Virtual supply chain model, 205-6
Visibility, 19-20, 55-56, 58
Volkswagen, 193-94
Volume, 10-11
von Neumann, John, 62

W

Wage arbitrage, 133
Wal-Mart
  acquisitions, 154
  in China, 189

Index

core competencies, 147
customers, 155-56
data volume, 5-6
demand methodology, 126
distribution center, xii, 152, 154
employment, 153
failures, 145, 155
growth, 154
import volume, xii
J-I-T practice, 145
origins, 121, 144
overseas market, 155
partnerships, 78-79
pull strategy, 123
retail sales, 11
RFID mandate, 14, 153-54
sales, 155-56
supply chain, 23, 147
supply chain strategy, 154
Walton, Sam, 144, 152
Warehouse
function of, 176
management system, 66, 95, 189
placement of, 176
precursors of, 88-89
replacement of, 177-78
Waste paper, xii
Waste removal, 56-57
Watson, Thomas, 185-86
Wealth of Nations, The, 117
Wearable computer, 214-15
Weiner, Norbert, 123
Weizmann Institute, 6
Welch, Sue, 149-50
Whitney, Eli, 118
Wireless communication, 78, 79
World Trade Organization, 190
Worst case scenario, 28-29

X-Y
Xybernaut, 214-15
Yanghan Deep Water Port, 162-63
Yum! Brands, 194

ABOUT THE AUTHOR

Robert A. Malone is the logistics editor for Forbes.com and has written columns for *Inbound Logistics* and an online column for *Managing Automation* for 10 years. He cofounded the Variflex Corporation, where he created "a variable speed goods and people mover," designed the movement of people and baggage for six airports, performed studies on the interaction of people and traffic at business activity centers, did a study for the U.S. Postal Service that predated electronic tracking and package modularization, and designed ATMs and bank branches for Citibank.

KAPLAN

With products serving children, adults, schools and businesses, Kaplan has an educational solution for every phase of learning.

KAPLAN — KIDS AND SCHOOLS

SCORE! Educational Centers offer individualized tutoring programs in reading, math, writing and other subjects for students ages 4-14 at more than 160 locations across the country. We help students achieve their academic potential while developing self-confidence and a love of learning.
www.escore.com

We also partner with schools and school districts through Kaplan K12 Learning Services to provide instructional programs that improve results and help all students achieve. We support educators with professional development, innovative technologies, and core and supplemental curriculum to meet state standards.
www.kaplank12.com

KAPLAN — TEST PREP AND ADMISSIONS

Kaplan Test Prep and Admissions prepares students for more than 80 standardized tests, including entrance exams for secondary school, college and graduate school, as well as English language and professional licensing exams. We also offer private tutoring and one-on-one admissions guidance.
www.kaptest.com

KAPLAN — HIGHER EDUCATION

Kaplan Higher Education offers postsecondary programs in fields such as business, criminal justice, health care, education, and information technology through more than 70 campuses in the U.S. and abroad, as well as online programs through Kaplan University and Concord Law School.
www.khec.com
www.kaplan.edu
www.concordlawschool.edu

KAPLAN — PROFESSIONAL

If you are looking to start a new career or advance in your field, Kaplan Professional offers training to obtain and maintain professional licenses and designations in the accounting, financial services, real estate and technology industries. We also work with businesses to develop solutions to satisfy regulatory mandates for tracking and compliance.
www.kaplanprofessional.com

Kaplan helps individuals achieve their educational and career goals. We build futures one success story at a time.